Very truly your friend,
Wm. Wells Brown.

My Southern Home:

OR,

THE SOUTH AND ITS PEOPLE.

BY

WM. WELLS BROWN, M.D.

" Go, little book, from this thy solitude!
I cast thee on the waters — go thy ways!
And if, as I believe, thy vein be good,
The world will find thee after many days."— *Southey.*

NEGRO UNIVERSITIES PRESS
NEW YORK

124466

Originally published in 1880
by A. G. Brown & Co., Publishers, Boston

Reprinted 1969 by
Negro Universities Press
A DIVISION OF GREENWOOD PUBLISHING CORP.
NEW YORK

SBN 8371-2012-8

PRINTED IN UNITED STATES OF AMERICA

PREFACE.

No attempt has been made to create heroes or heroines, or to appeal to the imagination or the heart.

The earlier incidents were written out from the author's recollections. The later sketches here given, are the results of recent visits to the South, where the incidents were jotted down at the time of their occurrence, or as they fell from the lips of the narrators, and in their own unadorned dialect.

BOSTON, May, 1880.

CONTENTS.

iv

XXV.

Oppressive Laws against Colored People. Revival of the Whipping Post. The Ku-Klux — their operations in Tennessee. Lynch Law triumphant.

XXVI.

Colored men as Servants, — their Improvidence. The love of Dress. Personal effort for Education.

XXVII.

Need of Combination. Should follow the Example set by the Irish, Germans, Italians, and Chinese who come to this country. Should patronize their own Race. Cadet Whittaker. Need of more Pluck.

XXVIII.

Total Abstinence from Intoxicating Drinks a necessary object for Self-Elevation. Intemperance and its Evils. Literary Associations. The Exodus. Emigration a Necessity. Should follow the Example of other Races. Professions and Trades needed.

XXIX.

Mixture of Races. The Anglo-Saxon. Isolated Races: The Negro — the Irish — the Coptic — the Jews — the Gypsies — the Romans, Mexicans, and Peruvians. Progressive Negroes, — Artists and Painters. Pride of Race.

GREAT HOUSE AT POPLAR FARM.

MY SOUTHERN HOME.

CHAPTER I.

TEN miles north of the city of St. Louis, in the State of Missouri, forty years ago, on a pleasant plain, sloping off toward a murmuring stream, stood a large frame-house, two stories high; in front was a beautiful lake, and, in the rear, an old orchard filled with apple, peach, pear, and plum trees, with boughs untrimmed, all bearing indifferent fruit. The mansion was surrounded with piazzas, covered with grape-vines, clematis, and passion flowers; the Pride of China mixed its oriental-looking foliage with the majestic magnolia, and the air was redolent with the fragrance of buds peeping out of every nook, and nodding upon you with a most unexpected welcome.

The tasteful hand of art, which shows itself in the grounds of European and New-England villas, was not seen there, but the lavish beauty and harmonious disorder of nature was permitted to take its own course, and exhibited a want of taste so commonly witnessed in the sunny South.

The killing effects of the tobacco plant upon the lands of "Poplar Farm," was to be seen in the rank growth of the brier, the thistle, the burdock, and the jimpson weed, showing themselves wherever the strong arm of the bondman had not kept them down.

Dr. Gaines, the proprietor of "Poplar Farm," was a good-humored, sunny-sided old gentleman, who, always feeling happy himself, wanted everybody to enjoy the same blessing. Unfortunately for him, the Doctor had been born and brought up in Virginia, raised in a family claiming to be of the "F. F. V.'s," but, in reality, was comparatively poor. Marrying Mrs. Sarah Scott Pepper, an accomplished widow lady of medium fortune, Dr. Gaines emigrated to Missouri, where he became a leading man in his locality.

Deeply imbued with religious feeling of the Calvinistic school, well-versed in the Scriptures, and having an abiding faith in the power of the Gospel to regenerate the world, the Doctor took great pleasure in presenting his views wherever his duties called him.

As a physician, he did not rank very high, for it was currently reported, and generally believed, that the father, finding his son unfit for mercantile business, or the law, determined to make him either a clergyman or a physician. Mr. Gaines, Senior, being somewhat superstitious, resolved not to settle the question too rashly in regard to the son's profession, therefore, it is said, flipped a cent, feeling that "heads or tails" would be a better omen than his own judgment in the matter. Fortunately for the cause of religion, the head turned up in favor of the medical profession.   Nevertheless, the son often said that he believed God had destined him for the *sacred calling*, and devoted much of his time in exhorting his neighbors to seek repentance.

Most planters in our section cared but little about the religious training of their slaves, regarding them as they did their cattle, — an investment, the return of which was only to be considered in dollars and cents.   Not so, however, with Dr. John Gaines, for he took special pride in looking after the spiritual welfare of his slaves, having them all in the "great house," at family worship, night and morning.

On Sabbath mornings, reading of the Scriptures, and explaining the same, generally occupied from one to two hours, and often till half of the negroes present were fast asleep.   The white members of the family did not take as kindly to the religious teaching of the doctor, as did the blacks.

For his Christian zeal, I had the greatest respect, for I always regarded him as a truly pious and conscientious man, willing at all times to give of his means the needful in spreading the Gospel.

Mrs. Sarah Gaines was a lady of considerable merit, well-educated, and of undoubted piety.   If she did not join heartily in her husband's religious enthusiasm, it was not for want of deep and genuine Christian feeling, but from the idea that he was of more humble origin than herself, and, therefore, was not a capable instructor.

This difference in birth, this difference in antecedents does much in the South to disturb family relations wherever it exists, and Mrs. Gaines, when wishing to show her contempt for the Doctor's opinions, would allude to her own parentage and birth in comparison to her husband's. Thus, once, when they were having a "family jar," she, with tears streaming down her cheeks, and wringing her hands, said, —

" My mother told me that I was a fool to marry a man so much beneath me, — one so much my inferior in society. And now you show it by hectoring and aggravating me all you can. But, never mind; I thank the Lord that He has given me religion and grace to stand it. Never mind, one of these days the Lord will make up His jewels, — take me home to glory, out of your sight, — and then I'll be devilish glad of it ! "

These scenes of unpleasantness, however, were not of everyday occurrence, and, therefore, the great house at the "Poplar Farm," may be considered as having a happy family.

Slave children, with almost an alabaster complexion, straight hair, and blue eyes, whose mothers were jet black, or brown, were often a great source of annoyance in the Southern household, and especially to the mistress of the mansion.

Billy, a quadroon of eight or nine years, was amongst the young slaves, in the Doctor's house, then being trained up for a servant. Any one taking a hasty glance at the lad would never suspect that a drop of negro blood coursed through his blue veins. A gentleman, whose acquaintance Dr. Gaines had made, but who knew nothing of the latter's family relations, called at the house in the Doctor's absence. Mrs. Gaines received the stranger, and asked him to be seated, and remain till the host's return. While thus waiting, the boy, Billy, had occasion to pass through the room. The stranger, presuming the lad to be a son of the Doctor, exclaimed, " How do you do?" and turning to the lady, said, "how much he looks like his father; I should have known it was the Doctor's son, if I had met him in Mexico !"

With flushed countenance and excited voice, Mrs. Gaines informed the gentleman that the little fellow was "only a slave and nothing more." After the stranger's departure, Billy was seen pulling up grass in the garden, with bare head, neck and shoulders, while the rays of the burning sun appeared to melt the child.

This process was repeated every few days for the purpose of giving the slave the color that nature had refused it. And yet, Mrs. Gaines was not considered a cruel woman, — indeed she was regarded as a kind-feeling mistress. Billy, however, a few days later, experienced a roasting far more severe than the one he had got in the sun.

The morning was cool, and the breakfast table was spread near the fireplace, where a newly-built fire was blazing up. Mrs. Gaines, being seated near enough to feel very sensibly the increasing flames, ordered Billy to stand before her.

The lad at once complied. His thin clothing

Gaines = Dr. John Young, his 1st master

giving him but little protection from the fire, the boy soon began to make up faces and to twist and move about, showing evident signs of suffering.

"What are you riggling about for?" asked the mistress. "It burns me," replied the lad; "turn round, then," said the mistress; and the slave commenced turning around, keeping it up till the lady arose from the table.

Billy, however, was not entirely without his crumbs of comfort. It was his duty to bring the hot biscuit from the kitchen to the great house table while the whites were at meal. The boy would often watch his opportunity, take a "cake" from the plate, and conceal it in his pocket till breakfast was over, and then enjoy his stolen gain. One morning Mrs. Gaines, observing that the boy kept moving about the room, after bringing in the "cakes," and also seeing the little fellow's pocket sticking out rather largely, and presuming that there was something hot there, said, "Come here." The lad came up; she pressed her hand against the hot pocket, which caused the boy to jump back. Again the mistress repeated, "Come here," and with the same result.

This, of course, set the whole room, servants and all, in a roar. Again and again the boy was ordered to "come up," which he did, each time jumping back, until the heat of the biscuit was exhausted, and then he was made to take it out and throw it into the yard, where the geese seized it and held a carnival over it. Billy was heartily laughed at by his companions in the kitchen and the quarters, and the large blister, caused by the hot biscuit, created merriment among the slaves, rather than sympathy for the lad.

Mrs. Gaines, being absent from home one day, and the rest of the family out of the house, Billy commenced playing with the shot-gun, which stood in the corner of the room, and which the boy supposed was unloaded; upon a corner shelf, just above the gun, stood a band-box, in which was neatly laid away all of Mrs. Gaines' caps and cuffs, which, in those days, were in great use.

The gun having the flint lock, the boy amused himself with bringing down the hammer and striking fire. By this action powder was jarred into the pan, and the gun, which was heavily charged with shot, was discharged, the contents passing through the band-box of caps, cutting them literally to pieces and scattering them over the floor.

Billy gathered up the fragments, put them in the box and placed it upon the shelf, — he alone aware of the accident.

A few days later, and Mrs. Gaines was expecting company; she called to Hannah to get her a clean cap. The servant, in attempting to take down the box, exclaimed: "Lor, misses, ef de rats ain't bin at dees caps an' cut 'em all to pieces, jes look here." With a degree of amazement not easily described the mistress beheld the fragments as they were emptied out upon the floor.

Just then a new idea struck Hannah, and she said: "I lay anything dat gun has been shootin' off."

"Where is Billy? Where is Billy?" exclaimed the mistress; "Where is Billy?" echoed Hannah; fearing that the lady would go into convulsions, I hastened out to look for the boy, but he was nowhere to be found; I returned only to find her weeping and wringing her hands, exclaiming, "O, I am ruined, I am ruined; the company's coming and not a clean cap about the house; O, what shall I do, what shall I do?"

I tried to comfort her by suggesting that the servants might get one ready in time; Billy soon made his appearance, and looked on with wonderment; and, when asked how he came to shoot off the gun, declared that he knew nothing about it · and "ef de gun went off, it was of its own accord." However, the boy admitted the snapping of the lock or trigger. A light whipping was all that he got, and for which he was well repaid by having an opportunity of telling how the "caps flew about the room when de gun went off."

Relating the event some time after in the quarters he said: "I golly, you had aughty seen dem caps fly, and de dust and smok' in de room. I thought de judgment day had come, sure nuff." On the arrival of the company, Mrs. Gaines made a very presentable appearance, although the caps and laces had been destroyed. One of the visitors on this occasion was a young Mr. Sarpee, of St. Louis, who, although above twenty-one years of age, had never seen anything of country life, and, therefore, was very anxious to remain over night, and go on a coon hunt. Dr. Gaines, being lame, could not accompany the gentleman, but sent Ike, Cato, and Sam; three of the most expert coon-hunters on the farm. Night came, and off went the young man and the boys on the coon hunt. The dogs scented game, after being about half an hour in the woods, to the great delight of Mr. Sarpee, who was armed with a double barrel pistol, which, he said, he carried both to "protect himself, and to shoot the coon."

The halting of the boys and the quick, sharp bark of the dogs announced that the game was "treed," and the gentleman from the city pressed forward with fond expectation of seeing the coon, and using his pistol. However, the boys soon raised the cry of "polecat, polecat; get out de way"; and at the same time, retreating as if they were afraid of an attack from the animal. Not so with Mr. Sarpee; he stood his ground. with pistol in hand, waiting to get a sight of the game. He was not long in suspense, for the white and black spotted creature soon made its appearance, at which the city gentleman opened fire upon the skunk, which attack was immediately answered by the animal, and in a manner that caused the young man to wish that he, too, had retreated with the boys. Such an odor, he had never before inhaled; and, what was worse, his face, head, hands and clothing was covered with the cause of the smell, and the gentleman, at once, said: "Come, let's go home; I've got enough of coon-hunting." But, didn't the boys enjoy the fun.

The return of the party home was the signal for a hearty laugh, and all at the expense of the city gentleman. So great and disagreeable **was** the smell, that the young man had to go to the barn, where his clothing was removed, and he submitted to the process of washing by the servants. Soap, scrubbing brushes, towels, indeed, everything was brought into requisition, but all to no purpose. The skunk smell was there, and was likely to remain. Both family and visitors were at the breakfast table, the next morning, except Mr. Sarpee. He was still in the barn, where he had slept the previous night. Nor did there seem to be any hope that he would be able to visit the house, for the smell was intolerable. The substitution of a suit of the Doctor's clothes for his own failed to remedy the odor.

Dinkie, the conjurer, was called in. He looked the young man over, shook his head in a knowing manner, and said it was a big job. Mr. Sarpee took out a Mexican silver dollar, handed it to the old negro, and told him to do his best. Dinkie smiled, and he thought that he could remove the smell.

His remedy was to dig a pit in the ground large enough to hold the man, put him in it, and cover him over with fresh earth; consequently, Mr. Sarpee was, after removing his entire clothing, buried, all except his head, while his clothing was served in the same manner. A servant held an umbrella over the unhappy man, and fanned him during the eight hours that he was there.

Taken out of the pit at six o'clock in the evening,

all joined with Dinkie in the belief that Mr. Sarpee "smelt sweeter," than when interred in the morning; still the smell of the "polecat" was there. Five hours longer in the pit, the following day, with a rub down by Dinkie, with his "Goopher," fitted the young man for a return home to the city.

I never heard that Mr. Sarpee ever again joined in a "coon hunt."

No description of mine, however, can give anything like a correct idea of the great merriment of the entire slave population on "Poplar Farm," caused by the "coon hunt." Even Uncle Ned, the old superannuated slave, who seldom went beyond the confines of his own cabin, hobbled out, on this occasion, to take a look at "de gentleman fum de city," while buried in the pit.

At night, in the quarters, the slaves had a merry time over the "coon hunt."

"I golly, but didn't de polecat give him a big dose?" said Ike.

"But how Mr. Sarpee did talk French to hissef when de ole coon peppered him," remarked Cato.

"He won't go coon huntin' agin, soon, I bet you," said Sam.

"De coon hunt," and "de gemmen fum de city," was the talk for many days.

CHAPTER II.

I HAVE already said that Dr. Gaines was a man of deep religious feeling, and this interest was not confined to the whites, for he felt that it was the Christian duty to help to save all mankind, white and black. He would often say, "I regard our negroes as given to us by an All Wise Providence, for their especial benefit, and we should impart to them Christian civilization." And to this end, he labored most faithfully.

No matter how driving the work on the plantation, whether seed-time or harvest, whether threatened with rain or frost, nothing could prevent his having the slaves all in at family prayers, night and morning. Moreover, the older servants were often invited to take part in the exercises. They always led the singing, and, on Sabbath mornings, were permitted to ask questions eliciting Scriptural explanations. Of course, some of the questions and some of the prayers were rather crude, and the effect, to an educated person, was rather to call forth laughter than solemnity.

Leaving home one morning, for a visit to the city, the Doctor ordered Jim, an old servant, to do some mowing in the rye-field; on his return, finding the rye-field as he had left it in the morning, he called Jim up, and severely flogged him without giving the man an opportunity of telling why the work had

12

been neglected. On relating the circumstance at the supper-table, the wife said,—

"I am very sorry that you whipped Jim, for I

TROPICAL LUXURIANCE.

took him to do some work in the garden, amongst my flower-beds."

To this the Doctor replied, "Never mind, I'll make it all right with Jim."

And sure enough he did, for that night, at prayers, he said, "I am sorry, Jim, that I corrected you, to-day, as your mistress tells me that she set you to work in the flower-garden. Now, Jim," continued he, in a most feeling manner, "I always want to do justice to my servants, and you know that I never abuse any of you intentionally, and now, to-night, I will let you lead in prayer."

Jim thankfully acknowledged the apology, and, with grateful tears, and an overflowing heart, accepted the situation; for Jim aspired to be a preacher, like most colored men, and highly appreciated an opportunity to show his persuasive powers; and that night the old man made splendid use of the liberty granted to him. After praying for everything generally, and telling the Lord what a great sinner he himself was, he said, —

"Now, Lord, I would specially ax you to try to save marster. You knows dat marster thinks he's mighty good; you knows dat marster says he's gwine to heaven; but Lord, I have my doubts; an' yet I want marster saved. Please to convert him over agin; take him, dear Lord, by de nap of de neck, and shake him over hell and show him his condition. But, Lord, don't let him fall into hell, jes let him see whar he ought to go to, but don't let him go dar. An' now, Lord, ef you jes save marster, I will give you de glory."

The indignation expressed by the doctor, at the close of Jim's prayer, told the old negro that for once he had overstepped the mark. " What do you mean, Jim, by insulting me in that manner? Asking the Lord to convert me over again. And praying that I might be shaken over hell. I have a great mind to tie you up, and give you a good correcting. If you ever make another such a prayer, I'll whip you well, that I will."

Dr. Gaines felt so intensely the duty of masters to their slaves that he, with some of his neighbors, inaugurated a religious movement, whereby the blacks at the Corners could have preaching once a fortnight, and that, too, by an educated white man. Rev. John Mason, the man selected for this work, was a heavy-set, fleshy, lazy man who, when entering a house, sought the nearest chair, taking possession of it, and holding it to the last.

He had been employed many years as a colporteur or missionary, sometimes preaching to the poor whites, and, at other times, to the slaves, for which service he was compensated either by planters, or by the dominant religious denomination in the section where he labored. Mr. Mason had carefully studied the character of the people to whom he was called to preach, and took every opportunity to shirk his duties, and to throw them upon some of the slaves, a large number of whom were always ready and willing to exhort when called upon.

We shall never forget his first sermon, and the profound sensation that it created both amongst masters and slaves, and especially the latter. After taking for his text, "He that knoweth his master's

will, and doeth it not, shall be beaten with many
stripes," he spoke substantially as follows : —

"Now when *correction* is given you, you either deserve it, or you do not deserve it.   But whether you
really deserve it or not, it is your duty, and Almighty
God requires that you bear it patiently.   You may,
perhaps, think that this is hard doctrine, but if you
consider it right you must needs think otherwise of it.
Suppose then, that you deserve correction, you cannot but say that it is just and right you should meet
with it.   Suppose you do not, or at least you do
not deserve so much, or so severe a correction for
the fault you have committed, you, perhaps, have
escaped a great many more, and are at last paid for
all.   Or suppose you are quite innocent of what is
laid to your charge, and suffer wrongfully in that
particular thing, is it not possible you may have
done some other bad thing which was never discovered, and that Almighty God, who saw you doing it,
would not let you escape without punishment one
time or another?   And ought you not, in such
a case, to give glory to Him, and be thankful that
he would rather punish you in this life for your
wickedness, than destroy your souls for it in the
next life?   But suppose that even this was not the
case (a case hardly to be imagined), and that you
have by no means, known or unknown, deserved
the correction you suffered, there is this great comfort in it, that if you bear it patiently, and leave
your cause in the hands of God, he will reward you
for it in heaven, and the punishment you suffer

unjustly here, shall turn to your exceeding great glory, hereafter."

At this point, the preacher hesitated a moment, and then continued, "I am now going to give you a description of hell, that awful place, that you will surely go to, if you don't be good and faithful servants.

"Hell is a great pit, more than two hundred feet deep, and is walled up with stone, having a strong, iron grating at the top. The fire is built of pitch pine knots, tar barrels, lard kegs, and butter firkins. One of the devil's imps appears twice a day, and throws about half a bushel of brimstone on the fire, which is never allowed to cease burning. As sinners die they are pitched headlong into the pit, and are at once taken up upon the pitchforks by the devil's imps, who stand, with glaring eyes and smiling countenances, ready to do their master's work."

Here the speaker was disturbed by the "Amens," "Bless God, I'll keep out of hell," "Dat's my sentiments," which plainly told him that he had struck the right key.

"Now," continued the preacher, "I will tell you where heaven is, and how you are to obtain a place there. Heaven is above the skies; its streets are paved with gold; seraphs and angels will furnish you with music which never ceases. You will all be permitted to join in the singing and you will be fed on manna and honey, and you will drink from fountains, and will ride in golden chariots."

"I am bound for hebben," ejaculated one.

"Yes, blessed God, hebben will be my happy home," said another.

These outbursts of feeling were followed, while the man of God stood with folded arms, enjoying the sensation that his eloquence had created.

After pausing a moment or two, the reverend man continued, "Are there any of you here who would rather burn in hell than rest in heaven? Remember that once in hell you can never get out. If you attempt to escape little devils are stationed at the top of the pit, who will, with their pitchforks, toss you back into the pit, *curchunk*, where you must remain forever. But once in heaven, you will be free the balance of your days." Here the wildest enthusiasm showed itself, amidst which the preacher took his seat.

A rather humorous incident now occurred which created no little merriment amongst the blacks, and to the somewhat discomfiture of Dr. Gaines, — who occupied a seat with the whites who were present.

Looking about the room, being unacquainted with the negroes, and presuming that all or nearly so were experimentally interested in religion, Mr. Mason called on Ike to close with prayer. The very announcement of Ike's name in such a connection called forth a broad grin from the larger portion of the audience.

Now, it so happened that Ike not only made no profession of religion, but was in reality the farthest off from the church of any of the servants at "Poplar Farm"; yet Ike was equal to the occasion, and at once responded, to the great amazement of his fellow slaves.

Ike had been, from early boyhood, an attendant upon whites, and he had learned to speak correctly for an uneducated person. He was pretty well versed in Scripture and had learned the principal prayer that his master was accustomed to make, and would often get his fellow-servants together at the barn on a rainy day and give them the prayer, with such additions and improvements as the occasion might suggest. Therefore, when called upon by Mr. Mason, Ike at once said, " Let us pray."

After floundering about for a while, as if feeling his way, the new beginner struck out on the well-committed prayer, and soon elicited a loud " amen," and " bless God for that," from Mr. Mason, and to the great amusement of the blacks. In his eagerness, however, to make a grand impression, Ike attempted to weave into his prayer some poetry on " Cock Robin," which he had learned, and which nearly spoiled his maiden prayer.

After the close of the meeting, the Doctor invited the preacher to remain over night, and accepting the invitation, we in the great house had an opportunity of learning more of the reverend man's religious views.

When comfortably seated in the parlor, the Doctor said, "I was well pleased with your discourse, I think the tendency will be good upon the servants."

" Yes," responded the minister, " The negro is eminently a religious being, more so, I think, than the white race. He is emotional, loves music, is wonderfully gifted with gab; the organ of alimentativeness largely developed, and is fond of approbation. I therefore try always to satisfy their vanity; call upon them to speak, sing, and pray, and sometimes to preach. That suits for this world. Then I give them a heaven with music in it, and with something to eat. Heaven without singing and food would be no place for the negro. In the cities, where many of them are free, and have control of their own time, they are always late to church meetings, lectures, or almost anything else. But let there be a festival or supper announced and they are all there on time."

"But did you know," said Dr. Gaines, "that the prayer that Ike made to-day he learned from me?"

"Indeed?" responded the minister.

"Yes, that boy has the imitative power of his race in a larger degree than most negroes that I have seen. He remembers nearly everything that he hears, is full of wit, and has most excellent judgment. However, his dovetailing the Cock Robin poetry into my prayer was too much, and I had to laugh at his adroitness."

The Doctor was much pleased with the minister, but Mrs. Gaines was not. She had great contempt for professional men who sprung from the lower class, and she regarded Mr. Mason as one to be endured but not encouraged. The Rev. Henry Pinchen was her highest idea of a clergyman. This gentleman was then expected in the neighborhood, and she made special reference to the fact, to her husband, when speaking of the "negro missionary," as she was wont to call the new-comer.

The preparation made, a few days later, for the reception of Mrs. Gaines' favorite spiritual adviser, showed plainly that a religious feast was near at hand, and in which the lady was to play a conspicuous part; and whether her husband was prepared to enter into the enjoyment or not, he would have to tolerate considerable noise and bustle for a week.

"Go, Hannah," said Mrs. Gaines, "and tell Dolly to kill a couple of fat pullets, and to put the biscuit to rise. I expect Brother Pinchen here this afternoon, and I want everything in order. Hannah, Hannah, tell Melinda to come here. We mistresses do have a hard time in this world; I don't see why the Lord should have imposed such heavy duties on us poor mortals. Well, it can't last always. I long to leave this wicked world, and go home to glory."

At the hurried appearance of the waiting maid the mistress said : "I am to have company this afternoon, Melinda. I expect Brother Pinchen here, and I want everything in order. Go and get one of my new caps, with the lace border, and get out my scolloped-bottomed dimity petticoat, and when you go out, tell Hannah to clean the white-handled knives, and see that not a speck is on them; for I want everything as it should be while Brother Pinchen is here."

Mr. Pinchen was possessed with a large share of the superstition that prevails throughout the South,

not only with the ignorant negro, who brought it
with him from his native land, but also by a great
number of well educated and influential whites.

On the first afternoon of the reverend gentleman's
visit, I listened with great interest to the following
conversation between Mrs. Gaines and her ministe-
rial friend.

"Now, Brother Pinchen, do give me some of your
experience since you were last here. It always does
my soul good to hear religious experience. It draws
me nearer and nearer to the Lord's side. I do love
to hear good news from God's people."

"Well, Sister Gaines," said the preacher, "I've
had great opportunities in my time to study the
heart of man. I've attended a great many camp-
meetings, revival meetings, protracted meetings,
and death-bed scenes, and I am satisfied, Sister
Gaines, that the heart of man is full of sin, and
desperately wicked. This is a wicked world, Sister
Gaines, a wicked world."

"Were you ever in Arkansas, Brother Pinchen?"
inquired Mrs. Gaines; "I've been told that the
people out there are very ungodly."

Mr. P. "Oh, yes, Sister Gaines. I once spent
a year at Little Rock, and preached in all the towns
round about there; and I found some hard cases out.
there, I can tell you. I was once spending a week
in a district where there were a great many horse
thieves, and, one night, somebody stole my pony.
Well, I knowed it was no use to make a fuss, so I
told Brother Tarbox to say nothing about it, and I'd

get my horse by preaching God's everlasting gospel: for I had faith in the truth, and knowed that my Saviour would not let me lose my pony. So the next Sunday I preached on horse-stealing, and told the brethren to come up in the evenin' with their hearts filled with the grace of God. So that night the house was crammed brimfull with anxious souls, panting for the bread of life. Brother Bingham opened with prayer, and Brother Tarbox followed, and I saw right off that we were gwine to have a blessed time. After I got 'em pretty well warmed up, I jumped on to one of the seats, stretched out my hands' and said: 'I know who stole my pony; I've found out; and you are in here tryin' to make people believe that you've got religion; but you ain't got it. And if you don't take my horse back to Brother Tarbox's pasture this very night, I'll tell your name right out in meetin' to-morrow night. Take my pony back, you vile and wretched sinner, and come up here and give your heart to God.' So the next mornin', I went out to Brother Tarbox's pasture, and sure enough, there was my bob-tail pony. Yes, Sister Gaines, there he was, safe and sound. Ha, ha, ha!"

Mrs. G. "Oh, how interesting, and how fortunate for you to get your pony! And what power there is in the gospel! God's children are very lucky. Oh, it is so sweet to sit here and listen to such good news from God's people? [*Aside.*] 'You Hannah, what are you standing there listening for, and neglecting your work? Never mind, my lady, I'll whip

you well when I am done here.   Go at your work
this moment, you lazy huzzy!   Never mind, I'll
whip you well.'   Come, do go on, Brother Pinchen,
with your godly conversation.   It is so sweet!   It
draws me nearer and nearer to the Lord's side."

Mr. P. "Well, Sister Gaines, I've had some
mighty queer dreams in my time, that I have.   You
see, one night I dreamed that I was dead and in
heaven, and such a place I never saw before.   As
soon as I entered the gates of the celestial empire, I
saw many old and familiar faces that I had seen
before.   The first person that I saw was good old
Elder Pike, the preacher that first called my attention to religion.   The next person I saw was Deacon
Billings, my first wife's father, and then I saw a host
of godly faces.   Why, Sister Gaines, you knowed
Elder Goosbee, didn't you?"

Mrs. G. "Why, yes; did you see him there?   He
married me to my first husband."

Mr. P. "Oh, yes, Sister Gaines, I saw the old
Elder, and he looked for all the world as if he had
just come out of a revival meetin'."

Mrs. G. "Did you see my first husband there,
Brother Pinchen?"

Mr. P. "No, Sister Gaines, I didn't see Brother
Pepper there; but I've no doubt but that Brother
Pepper was there."

Mrs. G. "Well, I don't know; I have my doubts.
He was not the happiest man in the world.   He was
always borrowing trouble about something or another.   Still, I saw some happy moments with Mr.

Pepper. I was happy when I made his acquaintance, happy during our courtship, happy a while after our marriage, and happy when he died." [*Weeps.*]

Hannah. "Massa Pinchen, did you see my ole man Ben up dar in hebben?"

Mr. P. "No, Hannah, I didn't go amongst the niggers."

Mrs. G. "No, of course Brother Pinchen didn't go among the blacks. What are you asking questions for? [*Aside.*] 'Never mind, my lady, I'll whip you well when I'm done here. I'll skin you from head to foot.' Do go on with your heavenly conversation, Brother Pinchen; it does my very soul good. This is indeed a precious moment for me. I do love to hear of Christ and Him crucified."

Mr. P. "Well, Sister Gaines, I promised Sister Daniels that I'd come over and see her a few moments this evening, and have a little season of prayer with her, and I suppose I must go."

Mrs. G. "If you must go, then I'll have to let you; but before you do, I wish to get your advice upon a little matter that concerns Hannah. Last week Hannah stole a goose, killed it, cooked it, and she and her man Sam had a fine time eating the goose; and her master and I would never have known anything about it if it had not been for Cato, a faithful servant, who told his master all about it. And then, you see, Hannah had to be severely whipped before she'd confess that she stole the goose. Next Sabbath is sacrament day, and I want to know if you think that Hannah is fit to go to the Lord's Supper, after stealing the goose." ˙

"Well, Sister Gaines," responded the minister, "that depends on circumstances. If Hannah has confessed that she stole the goose, and has been sufficiently whipped, and has begged her master's pardon, and begged your pardon, and thinks she will not do the like again, why then I suppose she can go to the Lord's Supper; for —

> 'While the lamp holds out to burn,
> The vilest sinner may return.'

But she must be sure that she has repented, and won't steal any more."

"Do you hear that, Hannah?" said the mistress. "For my part," continued she, "I don't think she's fit to go to the Lord's Supper; for she had no cause to steal the goose. We give our servants plenty of good food. They have a full run to the meal-tub, meat once a fortnight, and all the sour milk on the place, and I am sure that's enough for any one. I do think that our negroes are the most ungrateful creatures in the world. They aggravate my life out of me."

During this talk on the part of the mistress, the servant stood listening with careful attention, and at its close Hannah said : —

"I know, missis, dat I stole de goose, an' massa whip me for it, an' I confess it, an' I is sorry for it. But, missis, I is gwine to de Lord's Supper, next

Sunday, kase I ain't agwine to turn my back on my bressed Lord an' Massa for no old tough goose, dat I ain't." And here the servant wept as if she would break her heart.

Mr. Pinchen, who seemed moved by Hannah's words, gave a sympathizing look at the negress, and said, "Well, Sister Gaines, I suppose I must go over and see Sister Daniels; she'll be waiting for me."

After seeing the divine out, Mrs. Gaines said, "Now, Hannah, Brother Pinchen is gone, do you get the cowhide and follow me to the cellar, and I'll whip you well for aggravating me as you have to-day. It seems as if I can never sit down to take a little comfort with the Lord, without you crossing me. The devil always puts it into your head to disturb me, just when I am trying to serve the Lord. I've no doubt but that I'll miss going to heaven on your account. But I'll whip you well before I leave this world, that I will. Get the cowhide and follow me to the cellar."

In a few minutes the lady returned to the parlor, followed by the servant whom she had been correcting, and she was in a high state of perspiration, and, on taking a seat, said, "Get the fan, Hannah, and fan me; you ought to be ashamed of yourself to put me into such a passion, and cause me to heat myself up in this way, whipping you. You know that it is a great deal harder for me than it is for you. I have to exert myself, and it puts me all in a fever; while you have only to stand and take it."

On the following Sabbath, — it being Communion, — Mr. Pinchen officiated. The church being at the Corners, a mile or so from "Poplar Farm," the Communion wine, which was kept at the Doctor's, was sent over by the boy, Billy. It happened to be in the month of April, when the maple trees had been tapped, and the sap freely running.

Billy, while passing through the "sugar camp," or sap bush, stopped to take a drink of the sap, which looked inviting in the newly-made troughs. All at once it occurred to the lad that he could take a drink of the wine, and fill it up with sap. So, acting upon this thought, the youngster put the decanter to his mouth, and drank freely, lowering the beverage considerably in the bottle.

But filling the bottle with the sap was much more easily contemplated than done. For, at every attempt, the water would fall over the sides, none going in. However, the boy, with the fertile imagination of his race, soon conceived the idea of sucking his mouth full of the sap, and then squirting it into the bottle. This plan succeeded admirably, and the slave boy sat in the church gallery that day, and wondered if the communicants would have partaken so freely of the wine, if they had known that his mouth had been the funnel through which a portion of it had passed.

Slavery has had the effect of brightening the mental powers of the negro to a certain extent, especially those brought into close contact with the whites.

It is also a fact, that these blacks felt that when they could get the advantage of their owners, they had a perfect right to do so ; and the boy, Billy, no doubt, entertained a consciousness that he had done a very cunning thing in thus drinking the wine entrusted to his care.

CHAPTER III.

DR. GAINES' practice being confined to the planters and their negroes, in the neighbor-hood of "Poplar Farm," caused his income to be very limited from that source, and consequently he looked more to the products of his plantation for support. True, the new store at the Corners, to-gether with McWilliams' Tannery and Simpson's Distillery, promised an increase of population, and, therefore, more work for the physician. This was demonstrated very clearly by the Doctor's coming in one morning somewhat elated, and exclaiming : "Well, my dear, my practice is steadily increasing. I forgot to tell you that neighbor Wyman engaged me yesterday as his family physician ; and I hope that the fever and ague, which is now taking hold of the people, will give me more patients. I see by the New Orleans papers that the yellow fever is raging there to a fearful extent. Men of my pro-fession are reaping a harvest in that section this year. I would that we could have a touch of the yellow fever here, for I think I could invent a medicine that would cure it. But the yellow fever is a luxury that we medical men in this climate can't expect to enjoy; yet we may hope for the cholera."

"Yes," replied Mrs. Gaines, "I would be glad to see it more sickly, so that your business might prosper. But we are always unfortunate. Everybody here seems to be in good health, and I am afraid they'll keep so. However, we must hope for the best. We must trust in the Lord. Providence may possibly send some disease amongst us for our benefit."

On going to the office the Doctor found the faithful servant hard at work, and saluting him in his usual kind and indulgent manner, asked, "Well, Cato, have you made the batch of ointment that I ordered?"

Cato. "Yes, massa; I dun made de intment, an' now I is making the bread pills. De tater pills is up on the top shelf."

Dr. G. "I am going out to see some patients. If any gentlemen call, tell them I shall be in this afternoon. If any servants come, you attend to them. I expect two of Mr. Campbell's boys over. You see to them. Feel their pulse, look at their tongues, bleed them, and give them each a dose of calomel. Tell them to drink no cold water, and to take nothing but water gruel."

Cato. "Yes, massa; I'll tend to 'em."

The negro now said, "I allers knowed I was a doctor, an' now de ole boss has put me at it; I muss change my coat. Ef any niggers comes in, I wants to look suspectable. Dis jacket don't suit a doctor; I'll change it."

Cato's vanity seemed at this point to be at its height, and having changed his coat, he walked up and down before the mirror, and viewed himself to his heart's content, and saying to himself, "Ah! now I looks like a doctor. N w I can bleed, pull teef, or cut off a leg. Oh, well, well! ef I ain't put de pill stuff an' de intment stuff togedder. By golly, dat ole cuss will be mad when he finds it out, won't he? Nebber mind, I'll make it up in pills, and when de flour is on dem, he won't know what's in' em; an' I'll make some new intment. Ah! yonder comes Mr. Campbell's Pete an' Ned; dem's de ones massa sed was comin'. I'll see ef I looks right. [_Goes to the looking-glass and views himself._] I 'em some punkins, ain't I? [_Knock at the door._] Come in." _Enter_ PETE _and_ NED.

Pete. "Whar is de Doctor?"

Cato. "Here I is; don't you see me?"

Pete. "But whar is de ole boss?"

Cato. "Dat's none you business. I dun tole you dat I is de doctor, an' dat's enuff."

Ned. "Oh, do tell us whar de Doctor is. I is almos' dead. Oh, me! oh, dear me! I is so sick." [_Horrible faces._]

Pete. "Yes, do tell us; we don't want to stan' here foolin."

Cato. "I tells you again dat I is de doctor. I larn de trade under massa."

Ned. " Oh ! well den ; give me somethin' to stop dis pain. Oh, dear me ! I shall die."

Cato. " Let me feel your pulse. Now, put out your tongue. You is berry sick. Ef you don't mine, you'll die. Come out in de shed, an' I'll bleed you. [*Taking them out and bleeding them.*] " Dar, now, take dese pills, two in de mornin', and two at night, and ef you don't feel better, double de dose. Now, Mr. Pete, what's de matter wid you?"

Pete. " I is got de cole chills, an' has a fever in de night."

" Come out in de shed, an' I'll bleed you," said Cato, at the same time viewing himself in the mirror, as he passed out. After taking a quart of blood, which caused the patient to faint, they returned, the black doctor saying, " Now, take dese pills, two in de mornin', and two at night, an' ef dey don't help you, double de dose. Ah ! I like to forget to feel your pulse, and look at your tongue. Put out your tongue. [*Feels his pulse.*] Yes, I tells by de feel ob your pulse dat I is gib you de right pills?"

Just then, Mr. Parker's negro boy Bill, with his hand up to his mouth, and evidently in great pain, entered the office without giving the usual knock at the door, and which gave great offence to the new physician.

" What you come in dat door widout knockin' for ? " exclaimed Cato.

Bill. " My toof ache so, I didn't tink to knock. Oh, my toof! my toof ! Whar is de Doctor?"

Cato. " Here I is ; don't you see me?"

Bill. "What! you de Doctor, you brack cuss! You looks like a doctor! Oh, my toof! my toof! Whar is de Doctor?"

Cato. "I tells you I is de doctor. Ef you don't believe me, ax dese men. I can pull your toof in a minnit."

Bill. "Well, den, pull it out. Oh, my toof! how it aches! Oh, my toof!" [*Cato gets the rusty turnkeys.*]

Cato. "Now lay down on your back."

Bill. "What for?"

Cato. "Dat's de way massa does."

Bill. "Oh, my toof! Well, den, come on." [*Lies down. Cato gets astraddle of Bill's breast, puts the turnkeys on the wrong tooth, and pulls — Bill kicks, and cries out*] — Oh, do stop! Oh, oh, oh! [*Cato pulls the wrong tooth — Bill jumps up.*]

Cato. "Dar, now, I tole you I could pull your toof for you."

Bill. Oh, dear me! Oh, it aches yet! Oh, me! Oh, Lor-e-massy! You dun pull de wrong toof. Drat your skin! ef I don't pay you for this, you brack cuss! [*They fight, and turn over table, chairs, and bench — Pete and Ned look on.*]

During the *melée*, Dr. Gaines entered the office, and unceremoniously went at them with his cane, giving both a sound drubbing before any explanation could be offered. As soon as he could get an opportunity, Cato said, "Oh, massa! he's to blame, sir, he's to blame. He struck me fuss."

Bill. "No, sir; he's to blame; he pull de wrong toof. Oh, my toof! oh, my toof!"

Dr. G. "Let me see your tooth. Open your

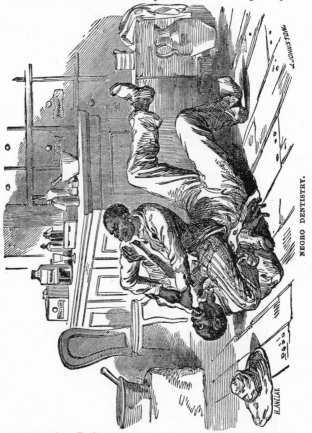

mouth. As I live, you've taken out the wrong tooth. I am amazed. I'll whip you for this; I'll whip you well. You're a pretty doctor. Now, lie down, Bill, and let him take out the right tooth; and if he makes a mistake this time, I'll cowhide him well. Lie down, Bill." [*Bill lies down, and Cato pulls the tooth.*] "There, now, why didn't you do that in the first place?"

Cato. "He wouldn't hole still, sir."

Bill. "I did hole still."

Dr. G. "Now go home, boys; go home."

"You've made a pretty muss of it, in my absence," said the Doctor. "Look at the table! Never mind, Cato; I'll whip you well for this conduct of yours to-day. Go to work now, and clear up the office."

As the office door closed behind the master, the irritated negro, once more left to himself, exclaimed, "Confound dat nigger! I wish he was in Ginny. He bite my finger, and scratch my face. But didn't I give it to him? Well, den, I reckon I did. [*He goes to the mirror, and discovers that his coat is torn — weeps.*] Oh, dear me! Oh, my coat — my coat is tore! Dat nigger has tore my coat. [*He gets angry, and rushes about the room frantic.*] Cuss dat nigger! Ef I could lay my hands on him, I'd tare him all to pieces, — dat I would. An' de old boss hit me wid his cane after dat nigger tore my coat. By golly, I wants to fight somebody. Ef ole massa should come in now, I'd fight him. [*Rolls up his sleeves.*] Let 'em come now, ef dey dare — ole massa, or anybody else; I'm ready for 'em."

Just then the Doctor returned and asked, "What's all this noise here?"

Cato. "Nuffin', sir; only jess I is puttin' things

to rights, as you tole me. I didn't hear any noise, except de rats."

Dr. G. "Make haste, and come in; I want you to go to town."

Once more left alone, the witty black said, "By golly, de ole boss like to cotch me dat time, didn't he? But wasn't I mad? When I is mad, nobody can do nuffin' wid me. But here's my coat tore to pieces. Cuss dat nigger! [*Weeps.*] Oh, my coat! oh, my coat! I rudder he had broke my head, den to tore my coat. Drat dat nigger! Ef he ever comes here agin, I'll pull out every toof he's got in his head — dat I will."

CHAPTER IV.

DURING the palmy days of the South, forty years ago, if there was one class more thoroughly despised than another, by the high-born, well-educated Southerner, it was the slave-trader who made his money by dealing in human cattle. A large number of the slave-traders were men of the North or free States, generally from the lower order, who, getting a little money by their own hard toil, invested it in slaves purchased in Virginia, Maryland, or Kentucky, and sold them in the cotton, sugar, or rice-growing States. And yet the high-bred planter, through mismanagement, or other causes, was compelled to sell his slaves, or some of them, at auction, or to let the "soul-buyer" have them.

Dr. Gaines' financial affairs being in an unfavorable condition, he yielded to the offers of a noted St. Louis trader by the name of Walker. This man was the terror of the whole South-west amongst the black population, bond and free, — for it was not unfrequently that even free colored persons were kidnapped and carried to the far South and sold. Walker had no conscientious scruples, for money was his God, and he worshipped at no other altar.

An uncouth, ill-bred, hard-hearted man, with no education, Walker had started at St. Louis as a dray-driver, and ended as a wealthy slave-trader. The day was set for this man to come and purchase his stock, on which occasion, Mrs. Gaines absented herself from the place; and even the Doctor, although alone, felt deeply the humiliation. For myself, I sat and bit my lips with anger, as the vulgar trader said to the faithful man, —

"Well, my boy, what's your name?"

Sam. "Sam, sir, is my name. .

Walk. "How old are you, Sam?"

Sam. "Ef I live to see next corn plantin' time I'll be twenty-seven, or thirty, or thirty-five, — I don't know which, sir."

Walk. "Ha, ha, ha! Well, Doctor, this is rather a green boy. Well, mer feller, are you sound?"

Sam. "Yes, sir, I spec I is."

Walk. "Open your mouth and let me see your teeth. I allers judge a nigger's age by his teeth, same as I dose a hoss. Ah! pretty good set of grinders. Have you got a good appetite?"

Sam. "Yes, sir."

Walk. "Can you eat your allowance?"

Sam. "Yes, sir, when I can get it."

Walk. "Get out on the floor and dance; I want to see if you are supple."

Sam. "I don't like to dance; I is got religion."

Walk. "Oh, ho! you've got religion, have you? That's so much the better. I likes to deal in the gospel. I think he'll suit me. Now, mer gal, what's your name?"

Sally. "I is Big Sally, sir."

Walk. "How old are you, Sally?"

Sally. "I don't know, sir; but I heard once dat I was born at sweet pertater diggin' time."

Walk. "Ha, ha, ha! Don't you know how old you are? Do you know who made you?"

Sally. "I hev heard who it was in de Bible dat made me, but I dun forget de gentman's name."

Walk. "Ha, ha, ha! Well, Doctor, this is the greenest lot of niggers I've seen for some time."

The last remark struck the Doctor deeply, for he had just taken Sally for debt, and, therefore, he was not responsible for her ignorance. And he frankly told him so.

"This is an unpleasant business for me, Mr. Walker," said the Doctor, "but you may have Sam for $1,000, and Sally for $900. They are worth all I ask for them. I never banter, Mr. Walker.

There they are; you can take them at that price,
or let them alone, just as you please."

Walk. "Well, Doctor, I reckon I'll take 'em;
but it's all they are worth. I'll put the handcuffs
on 'em, and then I'll pay you. I likes to go accor-
din' to Scripter. Scripter says ef eatin' meat will
offend your brother, you must quit it; and I say
ef leavin' your slaves without the handcuffs will
make 'em run away, you must put the handcuffs
on 'em. Now, Sam, don't you and Sally cry. I am
of a tender heart, and it allers makes me feel bad
to see people cryin'. Don't cry, and the first place
I get to, I'll buy each of you a great big *ginger cake*,
—that I will."

And with the last remark the trader took from a
small satchel two pairs of handcuffs, putting them
on, and with a laugh said: "Now, you look better
with the ornaments on."

Just then, the Doctor remarked,—"There comes
Mr. Pinchen." Walker, looking out and seeing the
man of God, said: "It is Mr. Pinchen, as I live;
jest the very man I wants to see." And as the reverend gentleman entered, the trader grasped his
hand, saying: "Why, how do you do, Mr. Pinchen?
What in the name of Jehu brings you down here to
Muddy Creek? Any camp-meetins, revival meetins,
death-bed scenes, or anything else in your line going
on down here? How is religion prosperin' now,
Mr. Pinchen? I always like to hear about religion.

Mr. Pin. "Well, Mr. Walker, the Lord's work
is in good condition everywhere now. I tell you,

Mr. Walker, I've been in the gospel ministry these thirteen years, and I am satisfied that the heart of man is full of sin and desperately wicked. This is a wicked world, Mr. Walker, a wicked world, and we ought all of us to have religion. Religion is a good thing to live by, and we all want it when we die. Yes, sir, when the great trumpet blows, we ought to be ready. And a man in your business of

REV. HENRY PINCHEN.

buying and selling slaves needs religion more than anybody else, for it makes you treat your people as you should. Now, there is Mr. Haskins, — he is a slave-trader, like yourself. Well, I converted him. Before he got religion, he was one of the worst men to his niggers I ever saw; his heart was as hard as stone. But religion has made his heart as soft as a piece of cotton. Before I converted him he would sell husbands from their wives, and seem to take delight in it; but now he won't sell a man from his wife, if he can get any one to buy both of them together. I tell you, sir, religion has done a wonderful work for him."

Walk. "I know, Mr. Pinchen, that I ought to have religion, and I feel that I am a great sinner; and whenever I get with good pious people like you and the Doctor, it always makes me feel that I am a desperate sinner. I feel it the more, because I've got a religious turn of mind. I know that I would be happier with religion, and the first spare time I get, I am going to try to get it. I'll go to a protracted meeting, and I won't stop till I get religion."

The departure of the trader with his property left a sadness even amongst the white members of the family, and special sympathy was felt for Hannah for the loss of her husband by the sale. However, Mrs. Gaines took it coolly, for as Sam was a field hand, she had often said she wanted her to have one of the house servants, and as Cato was without a wife, this seemed to favor her plans. Therefore, a week later, as Hannah entered the sitting-room one evening, she said to her: — "You need not tell me, Hannah, that you don't want another husband, I know better. Your master has sold Sam, and he's gone down the river, and you'll never see him again. So go and put on your calico dress, and meet me in the kitchen. I intend for you to *jump the broomstick* with Cato. You need not tell me you don't want another man. I know there's no woman living that can be happy and satisfied without a husband."

Hannah said: "Oh, missis, I don't want to jump de broomstick wid Cato. I don't love Cato; I can't love him."

Mrs. G. "Shut up, this moment! What do you know about love? I didn't love your master when I married him, and people don't marry for love now. So go and put on your calico dress, and meet me in the kitchen."

As the servant left for the kitchen, the mistress remarked: "I am glad that the Doctor has sold Sam, for now I'll have her marry Cato, and I'll have them both in the house under my eyes."

As Hannah entered the kitchen, she said: "Oh, Cato, do go and tell missis dat you don't want to jump de broomstick wid me, — dat's a good man. Do, Cato; kase I nebber can love you. It was only las week dat massa sold my Sammy, and I don't want any udder man. Do go tell missis dat you don't want me." To which Cato replied: "No, Hannah, I ain't a-gwine to tell missis no such thing, kase I does want you, and I ain't a-gwine to tell a lie for you ner nobody else. Dar, now you's got it! I don't see why you need to make so much fuss. I is better lookin' den Sam; an' I is a house servant, an' Sam was only a fiel hand; so you ought to feel proud of a change. So go and do as missis tells you."

As the woman retired, the man continued: "Hannah needn't try to get me to tell a lie; I ain't a-gwine

to do it, kase I dose want her, an' I is bin wantin'
her dis long time, an' soon as massa sold Sam, I
knowed I would get her. By golly, I is gwine to
be a married man. Won't I be happy? Now, ef I
could only jess run away from ole massa, an' get to
Canada wid Hannah, den I'd show 'em who I was.
Ah! dat reminds me of my song 'bout ole massa
and Canada, an' I'll sing it. Dis is my moriginal
hyme. It comed into my head one night when I was
fass asleep under an apple tree, looking up at de
moon."

While Hannah was getting ready for the nuptials,
Cato amused himself by singing —

> De happiest day I ever did see,
>   I'm bound fer my heavenly home,
> When missis give Hannah to me,
>   Through heaven dis chile will roam.

CHORUS. — Go away, Sam, you can't come a-nigh me,
>   Gwine to meet my friens in hebben,
>   Hannah is gwine along;
>   Missis ses Hannah is mine,
>   So Hannah is gwine along.

CHORUS, *repeated.*

> Father Gabriel, blow your horn,
>   I'll take wings and fly away,
> Take Hannah up in the early morn,
>   An' I'll be in hebben by de break of day.

CHORUS. — Go away, Sam, you can't come a-nigh mè,
>   Gwine to meet my friens in hebben,
>   Hannah is gwine along;
>   Missis ses Hannah is mine,
>   So Hannah is gwine along.

Mrs. Gaines, as she approached the kitchen, heard the servant's musical voice and knew that he was in high glee; entering, she said, "Ah! Cato, you're ready, are you? Where is Hannah?"

Cato. "Yes, missis; I is bin waitin' dis long time. Hannah has bin here tryin' to swade me to tell you dat I don't want her; but I telled her dat you sed I must jump de broomstick wid her, an' I is gwine to mind you."

Mrs. G. "That's right, Cato; servants should always mind their masters and mistresses, without asking a question."

Cato. "Yes, missis, I allers dose what you and massa tells me, an' axes nobody."

While the mistress went in search of Hannah, Dolly came in saying, "Oh, Cato, do go an' tell missis dat you don't want Hannah. Don't yer hear how she's whippin' her in de cellar? Do go an' tell missis dat you don't want Hannah, and den she'll stop whippin' her."

Cato. "No, Dolly, I ain't a gwine to do no such a thing, kase ef I tell missis dat I don't want Hannah, den missis will whip me; an' I ain't a-gwine to be whipped fer you, ner Hannah, ner nobody else. No, I'll jump the broomstick wid every woman on de place, ef missis wants me to, before I'll be whipped."

Dolly. "Cato, ef I was in Hannah's place, I'd see you in de bottomless pit before I'd live wid you, you great, big, wall-eyed, empty-headed, knock-kneed fool. You're as mean as your devilish old missis."

Cato. "Ef you don't quit dat busin' me, Dolly, I'll tell missis as soon as she comes in, an' she'll whip you, you know she will."

As Mrs. Gaines entered she said, "You ought to be ashamed of yourself, Hannah, to make me fatigue myself in this way, to make you do your duty. It's very naughty in you, Hannah. Now, Dolly, you and Susan get the broom, and get out in the middle of the room. There, hold it a little lower — a little higher; there, that'll do. Now, remember that this is a solemn occasion; you are going to jump into matrimony. Now, Cato, take hold of Hannah's hand. There, now, why could n't you let Cato take hold of your hand before? Now, get ready, and when I count three, do you jump. Eyes on the *broomstick!* All ready. One, two, three, and over you go. There, now you're husband and wife, and if you don't live happy together, it's your own fault; for I am sure there's nothing to hinder it. Now, Hannah, come up to the house, and I'll give you some whiskey, and you can make some apple-toddy, and you and Cato can have a fine time. Now, I'll go back to the parlor."

Dolly. "I tell you what, Susan, when I get married, I is gwine to have a preacher to marry me. I ain't a-gwine to jump de broomstick. Dat will do for fiel' hands, but house servants ought to be 'bove dat."

Susan. "Well, chile, you can't spect any ting else from ole missis. She come from down in Carlina, from 'mong de poor white trash. She don't know any

better. You can't speck nothin' more dan a jump
from a frog. Missis says she is one ob de akastocacy; but she ain't no more of an akastocacy dan I
is. Missis says she was born wid a silver spoon in
her mouf; ef she was, I wish it had a-choked her,
dat' what I wish."

The mode of jumping the broomstick was the
general custom in the rural districts of the South,
forty years ago; and, as there was no law whatever
in regard to the marriage of slaves, this custom had
as binding force with the negroes, as if they had
been joined by a clergyman; the difference being
the one was not so high-toned as the other. Yet, it
must be admitted that the blacks always preferred
being married by a clergyman.

CHAPTER V.

DR. GAINES and wife having spent the heated
season at the North, travelling for pleasure
and seeking information upon the mode of agriculture practised in the free States, returned home
filled with new ideas which they were anxious to
put into immediate execution, and, therefore, a rad-
ical change was at once commenced.

Two of the most interesting changes proposed,
were the introduction of a plow, which was to take
the place of the heavy, unwieldy one then in use,

and a washing-machine, instead of the hard hand-rubbing then practised. The first called forth much criticism amongst the men in the field, where it was christened the "Yankee Dodger," and during the first half a day of its use, it was followed by a large number of the negroes, men and women wondering at its superiority over the old plow, and wanting to know where it was from.

But the excitement in the kitchen, amongst the women, over the washing-machine, threw the novelty of the plow entirely in the shade.

"An' so dat tub wid its wheels an' fixin' is to do de washin', while we's to set down an' look at it," said Dolly, as ten or a dozen servants stood around the new comer, laughing and making fun at its ungainly appearance.

"I don't see why massa didn't buy a woman, out dar whar de ting was made, an' fotch 'em along, so she could learn us how to wash wid it," remarked Hannah, as her mistress came into the kitchen to give orders about the mode of using the "washer."

"Now, Dolly," said the mistress, "we are to have new rules, hereafter, about the work. While at the North, I found that the women got up at four o'clock, on Monday mornings, and commenced the washing, which was all finished, and out on the lines, by nine o'clock. Now, remember that, hereafter, there is to be no more washing on Fridays, and ironing on Saturdays, as you used to do. And instead of six of you great, big women to do the washing, two of you with the 'washer,' can do the work." And out she went, leaving the negroes to the contemplation of the future.

" I wish missis had stayed at home, 'stead of goin' round de world, bringin' home new rules. Who she tinks gwine to get out of bed at four o'clock in de mornin', kase she fotch home dis wash-box," said Dolly, as she gave a knowing look at the other servants.

" De Lord knows dat dis chile ain't a-gwine to git out of her sweet bed at four o'clock in de mornin', for no body; you hears dat, don't you?" remarked Winnie, as she gave a loud laugh, and danced out of the room.

Before the end of the week, Peter had run the new plow against a stump, and had broken it beyond the possibility of repair.

When the lady arose on Monday morning, at half-past nine, her usual time, instead of finding the washing out on the lines, she saw, to her great disappointment, the inside works of the "washer" taken out, and Dolly, the chief laundress, washing away with all her power, in the old way, rubbing with her hands, the perspiration pouring down her black face.

" What have you been doing, Dolly, with the ' washer?'" exclaimed the mistress, as she threw up her hands in astonishment.

" Well, you see, missis," said the servant, "dat merchine won't work no way. I tried it one way, den I tried it an udder way, an' still it would not work. So, you see, I got de screw-driver an' I took it to pieces. Dat's de reason I ain't got along faster wid de work."

Mrs. Gaines returned to the parlor, sat down, and had a good cry, declaring her belief that " negroes could not be made white folks, no matter what you should do with them."

Although the " patent plow " and the " washer " had failed, Dr. and Mrs. Gaines had the satisfaction of knowing that one of their new ideas was to be put into successful execution in a few days.

While at the North, they had eaten at a farm-house, some new cheese, just from the press, and on speaking of it, she was told by old Aunt Nancy, the black *mamma* of the place, that she understood all about making cheese. This piece of information gave general satisfaction, and a cheese-press was at once ordered from St. Louis.

The arrival of the cheese-press, the following week, was the signal for the new sensation. Nancy was at once summoned to the great house for the purpose of superintending the making of the cheese. A prouder person than the old negress could scarcely have been found. Her early days had been spent on the eastern shores of Maryland, where the blacks have an idea that they are, by nature, superior to their race in any other part of the habitable globe. Nancy had always spoken of the Kentucky and Missouri negroes as "low brack trash," and now, that all were to be passed over, and the only Mary-lander on the place called in upon this "great occasion," her cup of happiness was filled to the brim.

"What do you need, besides the cheese-press, to make the cheese with, Nancy?" inquired Mrs. Gaines, as the old servant stood before her, with her hands resting upon her hips, and looking at the half-dozen slaves who loitered around, listening to what was being said.

"Well, missis," replied Nancy, "I mus' have a runnet."

"What's a runnet?" inquired Mrs. Gaines.

"Why, you see, missis, you's got to have a sheep killed, and get out of it de maw, an' dat's what's called de runnet. An' I puts dat in de milk, an' it curdles the milk so it makes cheese."

"Then I'll have a sheep killed at once," said the mistress, and orders were given to Jim to kill the sheep. Soon after the sheep's carcass was distributed amongst the negroes, and " de runnet," in the hands of old Nancy.

That night there was fun and plenty of cheap talk in the negro quarters and in the kitchen, for it had been discovered amongst them that a calf's runnet, and not a sheep's, was the article used to curdle the milk for making cheese.

The laugh was then turned upon Nancy, who, after listening to all sorts of remarks in regard to her knowledge of cheese-making, said, in a triumphant tone, suiting the action to the words, —

"You niggers tink you knows a heap, but you don't know as much as you tink. When de sheep is killed, I knows dat you niggers would git de meat to eat. I knows dat."

·With this remark Nancy silenced the entire group. Then putting her hand a-kimbo, the old woman sarcastically exclaimed: "To-morrow you'll all have calf's meat for dinner, den what will you have to say 'bout old Nancy?" Hearing no reply, she said : "Whar is you smart niggers now? Whar is you, I ax you?"

"Well, den, ef Ant Nancy ain't some punkins, dis chile knows nuffin," remarked Ike, as he stood up at full length, viewing the situation, as if he had caught a new idea. "I allers tole yer dat Ant Nancy had moo in her head dan what yer catch out wid a fine-toof comb," exclaimed Peter.

"But how is you going to tell missis 'bout killin' de sheep?" asked Jim.

Nancy turned to the head man and replied: "De same mudder wit dat tole me to get some sheep fer you niggers will tell me what to do. De Lord always guides me through my troubles an' trials. Befoe I open my mouf, He always fills it."

The following day Nancy presented herself at the great house door, and sent in for her mistress. On the lady's appearing, the servant, putting on a knowing look, said : "Missis, when de moon is cold an' de water runs high in it, den I have to put calf's runnet in de milk, instead of sheep's. So, lass night, I see dat de moon is cold an' de water is runnin' high."

"Well, Nancy," said the mistress, "I'll have a calf killed at once, for I can't wait for a warm moon. Go and tell Jim to kill a calf immediately, for I must not be kept out of cheese much longer." On Nancy's return to the quarters, old Ned, who was past work, and who never did anything but eat, sleep and talk, heard the woman's explanation, and clapping his wrinkled hands exclaimed : "Well den, Nancy, you is wof moo den all de niggers on dis place, fer you gives us fresh meat ebbry day."

After getting the right runnet, and two weeks' work on the new cheese, a little, soft, sour, hard-looking thing, appearing like anything but a cheese, was exhibited at "Poplar Farm," to the great amusement of the blacks, and the disappointment of the whites, and especially Mrs. Gaines, who had frequently remarked that her "mouth was watering for the new cheese."

No attempt was ever made afterwards to renew the cheese-making, and the press was laid under the shed, by the side of the washing machine and the patent plow. While we had three or four trustworthy and faithful servants, it must be admitted that most of the negroes on "Poplar Farm" were always glad to shirk labor, and thought that to deceive the whites was a religious duty.

Wit and religion has ever been the negro's forte while in slavery. Wit with which to please his master, or to soften his anger when displeased, and religion to enable him to endure punishment when inflicted.

Both Dr. and Mrs. Gaines were easily deceived by their servants. Indeed, I often thought that Mrs. Gaines took peculiar pleasure in being misled

by them; and even the Doctor, with his long experience and shrewdness, would allow himself to be
carried off upon almost any pretext. For instance,
when he retired at night, Ike, his body servant,
would take his master's clothes out of the room,
brush them off and return them in time for the
Doctor to dress for breakfast. There was nothing

new material

MRS. SARAH PEPPER GAINES.

in this out of the way; but the master would often
remark that he thought Ike brushed his clothes too
much, for they appeared to wear out a great deal
faster than they had formerly. Ike, however, attrib-
uted the wear to the fact that the goods were wanting in soundness. Thus the master, at the advice of
his servant, changed his tailor.

About the same time the Doctor's watch stopped at night, and when taken to be repaired, the watch-maker found it badly damaged, which he pronounced had been done by a fall. As the Doctor was always very careful with his time-piece, he could in no way account for the stoppage. Ike was questioned as to his handling of it, but he could throw no light upon the subject. At last, one night about twelve o'clock, a message came for the Doctor to visit a patient who had a sudden attack of cholera morbus. The faithful Ike was nowhere to be found, nor could any traces of the Doctor's clothes be discovered. Not even the watch, which was always laid upon the mantle-shelf, could be seen anywhere.

It seemed clear that Ike had run away with his master's daily wearing apparel, watch and all. Yes, and further search showed that the boots, with one heel four inches higher than the other, had also dis-appeared. But go, the Doctor must; and Mrs. Gaines and all of us went to work to get the Doctor ready.

While Cato was hunting up the old boots, and Hannah was in the attic getting the old hat, Jim returned from the barn and informed his master that the sorrel horse, which he had ordered to be saddled, was nowhere to be found; and that he had got out the bay mare, and as there was no saddle on the place, Ike having taken the only one, he, Jim, had put the buffalo robe on the mare.

It was a bright moonlight night, and to see the Doctor on horseback without a saddle, dressed in his castaway suit, was, indeed, ridiculous in the extreme. However, he made the visit, saved the patient's life, came home and went snugly to bed. The following morning, to the Doctor's great surprise, in walked Ike, at his usual time, with the clothes in one hand and the boots nicely blacked in the other. The faithful slave had not seen any of the other servants, and consequently did not know of the master's discomfiture on the previous night.

"Were any of the servants off the place last night?" inquired the Doctor, as Ike laid the clothes carefully on a chair, and was setting down the boots.

"No, I speck not," answered Ike.

"Were you off anywhere last night?" asked the master.

"No, sir," replied the servant.

"What! not off the place at all?" inquired the Doctor sharply. Ike looked confused and evidently began to "smell a mice."

"Well, massa, I was not away only to step over to de prayer-meetin' at de Corners, a little while, dat's all," said Ike.

"Where's my watch?" asked the Doctor.

"I speck it's on de mantleshelf dar, whar I put it lass night, sir," replied Ike, and at the same time reached to the time-piece, where he had laid it a moment before, and holding it up triumphantly, "Here it is, sir, right where I left it lass night."

Ike was told to go, which he was glad to do. "What shall I do with that fellow?" said the Doctor to his wife, as the servant quitted the room.

Ike had scarcely reached the back yard when he met Cato, who told him of his absence on the previous night being known to his master. When Ike had heard all, he exclaimed, "Well, den ef de ole boss knows it, dis nigger is kotched sure as you is born."

"I would not be in your shoes, Ike, fer a heap, dis mornin'," said Cato.

"Well," replied Ike, "I thank de Lord dat I is got religion to stand it."

Dr. Gaines, as he dressed himself, found nothing out of the way until he came to look at the boots. The Doctor was lame from birth. Here he saw unmistakable evidence that the high heel had been taken off, and had been replaced by a screw put through the inside, and the seam waxed over. Dr. Gaines had often thought, when putting his boots on in the morning, that they appeared a little loose, and on speaking of it to his servant, the negro would attribute it to the blacking, which he said "made de lether stretch."

That morning when breakfast was over, and the negroes called in for family prayers, all eyes were upon Ike.

It has always appeared strange that the negroes should seemingly take such delight in seeing their fellow-servants in a "bad fix." But it is nevertheless true, and Ike's "bad luck" appeared to furnish sport for old and young of his own race. At the conclusion of prayers, the Doctor said, "Now, Ike, I want you to tell me the truth, and nothing but the truth, of your whereabouts last night, and why you wore away my clothes?"

"Well, massa," said Ike, "I'm gwine to tell you God's truth."

"That's what I want, Ike," remarked the master.

"Now," continued the negro, "I ware de clothes to de dance, kase you see, massa, I knowed dat you didn't want your body servant to go to de ball looking poorer dressed den udder gentmen's boys. So you see I had no clothes myself, so I takes yours. I had to knock the heel off de lame leg boot, so dat I could ware it. An' den I took 'ole Sorrel,' kase he paces so fass an' so easy. No udder hoss could get me to de city in time fer de ball, ceptin' 'ole Sorrel.' You see, massa, ten miles is a good ways to go after you is gone to bed. Now, massa, I hope you'll forgive me dis time, an' I'll never do so any moo."

During Ike's telling his story, his master kept his eyes rivetted upon him, and at its conclusion said: "You first told me that you were at the prayer-meeting at the Corners; what did you do that for?"

"Well, massa," replied Ike, "I knowed dat I ought to had gone to de prar-meetin', an' dat's de reason I said I was dar."

"And you're a pretty Christian, going to a dance, instead of your prayer-meeting. This is the fifth time you've fallen from grace," said the master.

"Oh, no," quickly responded Ike; "dis is only de fourf time dat I is back slid."

"But this is not the first time that you have taken my clothes and worn them. And there's my watch, you could not tell the time, what did you want with that?" said the Doctor.

"Yes, massa," replied Ike, "I'll tell de truth; I wore de clothes afore dis time, an' I take de watch too, an' I let it fall, an' dat's de reason it stop dat time. An' I know I could not tell de time by de watch, but I guessed at it, an' dat made de niggers star at me, to see me have a watch."

The announcement that Col. Lemmy was at the door cut short the further investigation of Ike's case. The Colonel was the very opposite to Dr. Gaines, believing that there was no good in the negro, except to toil, and feeling that all religious efforts to better the condition of the race was time thrown away.

The Colonel laughed heartily as the Doctor told how Ike had worn his clothes. He quickly inquired if the servant had been punished, and when informed that he had not, he said: "The lash is worth more than all the religion in the world. Your boy, Ike, with the rest of the niggers around here, will go to a prayer meetin' and will tell how good they feel or how bad they feel, just as it may suit the case. They'll cry, groan, clap their hands, pat their feet, worry themselves into a lather of sweat, sing,

> I'm a-gwine to keep a-climbin' high,
>   See de hebbenly land;
> Till I meet dem er angels in a de sky
>   See de hebbenly lan'.
>
> Dem pooty angels I shall see,
>   See de hebbenly lan';
> Why don't de debbil let a-me be,
>   See de hebbenly lan'.

"Yes, Doctor; these niggers will pray till twelve o'clock at night; break up their meeting and go home shouting and singing, 'Glory hallelujah!' and every-darned one of them will steal a chicken, turkey, or pig, and cry out 'Come down, sweet chariot, an' carry me home to hebben!' yes, and still continue to sing till they go to sleep. You may give your slaves religion, and I'll give mine the whip, an' I'll bet that I'll get the most tobacco and hemp out of the same number of hands."

"I hardly think," said the Doctor, after listening attentively to his neighbor, "that I can let Ike pass without some punishment. Yet I differ with you in regard to the good effects of religion upon all classes, more especially our negroes, for the African is preeminently a religious being; with them, I admit, there is considerable superstition. They have a permanent belief in good and bad luck, ghosts, fortune-telling, and the like; but we whites are not entirely free from such notions."

At the last sentence or two, the Colonel's eyes sparkled, and he began to turn pale, for it was well known that he was a firm believer in ghosts and fortune-telling.

"Now, Doctor," said Col. Lemmy, "every sensible man must admit the fact that ghosts exist, and that there is nothing in the world truer than that the future can be told. Look at Mrs. McWilliams' lawsuit with Major Todd. She went to old Frank, the nigger fortune-teller, and asked him which lawyer she should employ. The old man gazed at her for

a moment or two, and said, ' missis, you's got your
mind on two lawyers, — a big man and a little man.
Ef you takes de big man, you loses de case; ef
you takes de little man, you wins de case.' Sure
enough, she had in contemplation the employment
of either McGuyer or Darby. The first is a large
man; the latter was, as you know, a small man.
So, taking the old negro's advice, she obtained the
services of John F. Darby, and gained the suit."

"Yes," responded the Doctor, "I have always
heard that the Widow McWilliams gained her case
by consulting old Frank."

"Why, Doctor," continued the Colonel, in an ani-
mated manner, "When the races were at St. Louis,
three years ago, I went to old Betty, the blind
fortune-teller, to see which horse was going to win;
and she said, 'Massa, bet your money on de gray
mare.' Well, you see, everybody thought that
Johnson's black horse would win, and piles of
money was bet on him. However, I bet one hundred dollars on the gray mare, and, to the utter
surprise of all, she won. When the race was over,
I was asked how I come to bet on the mare, when
everybody was putting their funds on the horse. I
then told them that I never risked my money on any
horse, till I found out which was going to win.

"Now, with regard to ghosts, just let me say to
you, Doctor, that I saw the ghost of the peddler
that was murdered over on the old road, just as
sure as you are born."

"Do you think so?" asked the Doctor.

"Think so! Why, I know it, just as well as I know that I see you now. He had his pack on his back; and it was in the daytime, no night-work about it. He looked at me, and I watched him till he got out of sight. But wasn't I frightened; it made the hair stand up on my head, I tell you."

"Did he speak to you?" asked the Doctor.

"Oh, no! he didn't speak, but he had a sorrowful look, and, as he was getting out of sight, he turned and looked over his shoulder at me."

Most of the superstition amongst the whites, in our section, was the result of their close connection with the blacks; for the servants told the most foolish stories to the children in the nurseries, and they learned more, as they grew older, from the slaves in the quarters, or out on the premises.

CHAPTER VI.

PROFITABLE and interesting amusements were always needed at the Corners, the nearest place to the "Poplar Farm." At the tavern, post-office, and the store, all the neighborhood assembled to read the news, compare notes, and to talk politics.

Shows seldom ventured to stop there, for want of sufficient patronage. Once in three months, however, they had a "Gander Snatching," which never failed to draw together large numbers of ladies as

well as gentlemen, the *elite*, as well as the common.
The getter-up of this entertainment would procure a
gander of the wild goose species. This bird had a
long neck, which was large as it rose above the
breast, but tapered gradually., for more than half the
length, until it became small and serpent-like in form,
terminating in a long, slim head, and peaked bill.
The head and neck of the gander was well-greased;
the legs were tied together with a strong cord, and
the bird was then fastened by its legs, to a swinging
limb of a tree. The *Snatchers* were to be on horseback, and were to start fifteen or twenty rods from
the gander, riding at full speed, and, as they passed
along under the bird, they had the right to pull his
head off if they could. To accelerate the speed of
the horses, a man was stationed a few feet from the
gander, with orders to give every horse a cut with
his whip, as he went by.

Sometimes the bird's head would be caught by ten
or a dozen before they would succeed in pulling it off,
which was necessary; often by the sudden jump of
the animal, or the rider having taken a little too much
wine, he would fall from his horse, which event would
give additional interest to the " Snatching."

The poor gander would frequently show far more
sagacity than its torturers. After having its head
caught once or twice, the gander would draw up its
head, or dodge out of the way. Sometimes the
snatcher would have in his hand a bit of sand-
paper, which would enable him to make a tighter
grasp. But this mode was generally considered

unfair, and, on one occasion, caused a duel in which both parties were severely wounded.

But the most costly and injurious amusement that the people in our section entered into was that of card-playing, a species of gambling too much indulged in throughout the entire South. This amusement causes much sadness, for it often occurs that gentlemen lose large sums at the gambling-table, frequently seriously embarrassing themselves, sometimes bringing ruin upon whole families.

Mr. Oscar Smith, residing near "Poplar Farm," took a trip to St. Louis, thence to New Orleans and back. On the steamer he was beguiled into gaming.

"Go call my boy, steward," said Mr. Smith, as he took his cards one by one from the table.

In a few moments a fine-looking, bright-eyed mulatto boy, apparently about fifteen years of age, was standing by his master's side at the table.

"I will see you and five hundred dollars better," said Smith, as his servant Jerry approached the table.

"What price do you set on that boy?" asked Johnson, as he took a roll of bills from his pocket.

"He will bring a thousand dollars, any day, in the New Orleans market," replied Smith.

"Then you bet the whole of the boy, do you?"

"Yes."

"I call you, then," said Johnson, at the same time spreading his cards out upon the table.

"You have beat me," said Smith, as soon as he saw the cards.

Jerry, who was standing on top of the table, with

the bank-notes and silver dollars round his feet, was now ordered to descend from the table.

"You will not forget that you belong to me," said

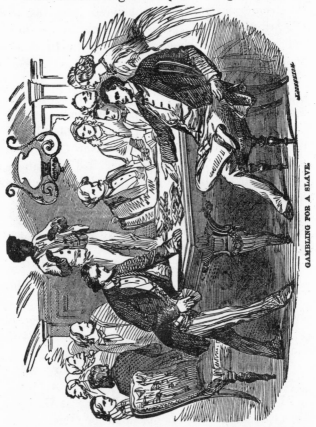

GAMBLING FOR A SLAVE.

Johnson, as the young slave was stepping from the table to a chair.

"No, sir," replied the chattel.

"Now go back to your bed, and be up in time to-morrow morning to brush my clothes and clean my boots, do you hear?"

"Yes, sir," responded Jerry, as he wiped the tears from his eyes.

As Mr. Smith left the gaming-table, he said: "I claim the right of redeeming that boy, Mr. Johnson. My father gave him to me when I came of age, and I promised not to part with him."

"Most certainly, sir, the boy shall be yours whenever you hand me over a cool thousand," replied Johnson.

The next morning, as the passengers were assembling in the breakfast saloons, and upon the guards of the vessel, and the servants were seen running about waiting upon or looking for their masters, poor Jerry was entering his new master's state-room with his boots.

The genuine wit of the negro is often a marvel to the whites, and this wit or humor, as it may be called, is brought out in various ways. Not unfrequently is it exhibited by the black, when he really means to be very solemn.

Thus our Sampey met Davidson's Joe, on the road to the Corners, and called out to him several times without getting an answer. At last, Joe, appearing much annoyed, stopped, looked at Sampey in an attitude of surprise, and exclaimed: "Ain't you got no manners? Whare's your eyes? Don't you see I is a funeral?"

It was not till then that Sampey saw that Joe had

a box in his arms, resembling a coffin, in which was a deceased negro child. The negro would often show his wit to the disadvantage of his master or mistress.

When visitors were at "Poplar Farm," Dr. Gaines would frequently call in Cato to sing a song or crack a joke, for the amusement of the company. On one occasion, requesting the servant to give a toast, at the same time handing the negro a glass of wine, the latter took the glass, held it up, looked at it, began to show his ivory, and said:

> " De big bee flies high,
>   De little bee makes de honey,
>   De black man raise de cotton,
>   An' de white man gets de money."

The same servant going to meeting one .Sabbath, was met on the road by Major Ben. O'Fallon, who was riding on horseback, with a hoisted umbrella to keep the rain off. The Major, seeing the negro trudging along bareheaded and with something under his coat, supposing he had stolen some article which he was attempting to hide, said, "What's that you've got under your coat, boy?"

"Nothin', sir, but my hat," replied the slave, and at the same time drawing forth a second-hand beaver.

"Is it yours?" inquired the Major.

"Yes, sir," was the quick response of the negro.

"Well," continued the Major, "if it is yours, why

don't you wear it and save your head from the rain?"

"Oh!" replied the servant, with a smile of seeming satisfaction, "de head belongs to massa an' de hat belongs to me. Let massa take care of his property, an' I'll take care of mine."

Dr. Gaines, while taking a neighbor out to the pig sty, to show him some choice hogs that he intended for the next winter's bacon, said to Dolly who was feeding the pigs: "How much lard do you think you can get out of that big hog, Dolly?"

The old negress scratched her wooly head, put on a thoughtful look, and replied, "I specks I can get a pail full, ef de pail aint too big."

"I reckon you can," responded the master.

The ladies are not without their recreation, the most common of which is snuff-dipping. A snuff-box or bottle is carried, and with it a very small stick or cane, which has been chewed at the end until it forms a small mop. The little dippers or sticks are sold in bundles for the use of the ladies, and can be bought simply cut in the requisite lengths or chewed ready for use. This the dipper moistens with saliva, and dips into the snuff-box, and then lifts the mop thus loaded inside the lips. In some parts they courteously hand round the snuff and dipper, or place a plentiful supply of snuff on the table, into which all the company may dip.

Amongst even the better classes of whites, the ladies would often assemble in considerable numbers, especially during revival meeting times, place a wash-dish in the middle of the room, all gather around it, commence snuff-dipping, and all using the wash-dish as a common spittoon.

Every well bred lady carries her own snuff-box and dipper. Generally during church service, where the clergyman is a little prosy, snuff-dipping is indispensible.

CHAPTER VII.

FORTY years ago, in the Southern States, superstition held an exalted place with all classes, but more especially with the blacks and uneducated, or poor, whites. This was shown more clearly in their belief in witchcraft in general, and the devil in particular. To both of these classes, the devil was a real being, sporting a club-foot, horns, tail, and a hump on his back.

The influence of the devil was far greater than that of the Lord. If one of these votaries had stolen a pig, and the fear of the Lord came over him, he would most likely ask the Lord to forgive him, but still cling to the pig. But if the fear of the devil came upon him, in all probability he would drop the pig and take to his heels.

In those days the city of St. Louis had a large number who had implicit faith in Voudooism. I once attended one of their midnight meetings. In the pale rays of the moon the dark outlines of a

large assemblage was visible, gathered about a small
fire, conversing in different tongues. They were
negroes of all ages, — women, children, and men.
Finally, the noise was hushed, and the assembled
group assumed an attitude of respect. They made
way for their queen, and a short, black, old negress
came upon the scene, followed by two assistants,
one of whom bore a cauldron, and the other, a box.

The cauldron was placed over the dying embers,
the queen drew forth, from the folds of her gown, a
magic wand, and the crowd formed a ring around
her. Her first act was to throw some substance on
the fire, the flames shot up with a lurid glare — now
it writhed in serpent coils, now it darted upward in
forked tongues, and then it gradually transformed
itself into a veil of dusky vapors. At this stage,
after a certain amount of gibberish and wild gesticulation from the queen, the box was opened, and
frogs, lizards, snakes, dog liver, and beef hearts
drawn forth and thrown into the cauldron. Then
followed more gibberish and gesticulation, when the
congregation joined hands, and began the wildest
dance imaginable, keeping it up until the men and
women sank to the ground from mere exhaustion.

In the ignorant days of slavery, there was a general belief that a horse-shoe hung over the door
would insure good luck. I have seen negroes, otherwise comparatively intelligent, refuse to pick up a
pin, needle, or other such object, dropped by a
negro, because, as they alleged, if the person who
dropped the articles had a spite against them, to

touch anything they dropped would voudou them, and make them seriously ill.

Nearly every large plantation, with any considerable number of negroes, had at least one, who laid claim to be a fortune-teller, and who was regarded with more than common respect by his fellow-slaves. Dinkie, a full-blooded African, large in frame, coarse featured, and claiming to be a descendant of a king in his native land, was the oracle on the "Poplar Farm." At the time of which I write, Dinkie was about fifty years of age, and had lost an eye, and was, to say the least, a very ugly-looking man.

No one in that section was considered so deeply immersed in voudooism, goopherism, and fortune-telling, as he. Although he had been many years in the Gaines family, no one could remember the time when Dinkie was called upon to perform manual labor. He was not sick, yet he never worked. No one interfered with him. If he felt like feeding the chickens, pigs, or cattle, he did so. Dinkie hunted, slept, was at the table at meal time, roamed through the woods, went to the city, and returned when he pleased, with no one to object, or to ask a question. Everybody treated him with respect. The whites, throughout the neighborhood, tipped their hats to the old one-eyed negro, while the policemen, or patrollers, permitted him to pass without a challenge. The negroes, everywhere, stood in mortal fear of "Uncle Dinkie." The blacks who saw him every day, were always thrown upon their good behavior, when in his presence. I once asked a negro why they appeared to be afraid of Dinkie. He looked at me, shrugged his shoulders, smiled, shook his head and said, —

"I ain't afraid of de debble, but I ain't ready to go to him jess yet." He then took a look around and behind, as if he feared some one would hear what he was saying, and then continued : "Dinkie's got de power, ser ; he knows things seen and unseen, an' dat's what makes him his own massa."

It was literally true, this man was his own master. He wore a snake's skin around his neck, carried a petrified frog in one pocket, and a dried lizard in the other.

A slave speculator once came along and offered to purchase Dinkie. Dr. Gaines, no doubt, thought it a good opportunity to get the elephant off his hands, and accepted the money. A day later, the trader returned the old negro, with a threat of a suit at law for damages.

A new overseer was employed, by Dr. Gaines, to take charge of "Poplar Farm." His name was Grove Cook, and he was widely known as a man of ability in managing plantations, and in raising a large quantity of produce from a given number of hands. Cook was called a "hard overseer." The negroes dreaded his coming, and, for weeks before his arrival, the overseer's name was on every slave's tongue.

Cook came, he called the negroes up, men and women ; counted them, looked them over as a purchaser would a drove of cattle that he intended to buy. As he was about to dismiss them he saw

Dinkie come out of his cabin. The sharp eye of the overseer was at once on him.

"Who is that nigger?" inquired Cook.

"That is Dinkie," replied Dr. Gaines.

"What is his place?" continued the overseer.

"Oh, Dinkie is a gentleman at large!" was the response.

"Have you any objection to his working?"

"None, whatever."

"Well, sir," said Cook, "I'll put him to work to-morrow morning."

Dinkie was called up and counted in.

At the roll call, the following morning, all answered except the conjurer; he was not there.

The overseer inquired for Dinkie, and was informed that he was still asleep.

"I will bring him out of his bed in a hurry," said Cook, as he started towards the negro's cabin. Dinkie appeared at his door, just as the overseer was approaching.

"Follow me to the barn," said the impatient driver to the negro. "I make it a point always to whip a nigger, the first day that I take charge of a farm, so as to let the hands know who I am. And, now, Mr. Dinkie, they tell me that you have not had your back tanned for many years; and, that being the case, I shall give you a flogging that you will never forget. Follow me to the barn." Cook started for the barn; but turned and went into his house to get his whip.

At this juncture, Dinkie gave a knowing look to

the other slaves, who were standing by, and said, "Ef he lays the weight ob his finger on me, you'll see de top of dat barn come off."

The reappearance of the overseer, with the large negro whip in one hand, and a club in the other, with the significant demand of "follow me," caused a deep feeling in the breast of every negro present.

Dr. Gaines, expecting a difficulty between his new driver and the conjurer, had arisen early, and was standing at his bedroom window looking on.

The news that Dinkie was to be whipped; spread far and near over the place, and had called forth men, women, and children. Even Uncle Ned, the old negro of ninety years, had crawled out of his straw, and was at his cabin door. As the barn doors closed behind the overseer and Dinkie, a death-like silence pervaded the entire group, who, instead of going to their labor, as ordered by the driver, were standing as if paralyzed, gazing intently at the barn, expecting every moment to see the roof lifted.

Not a word was spoken by anyone, except Uncle Ned, who smiled, shook his head, put on a knowing countenance, and said, "My word fer it, de oberseer ain't agwine to whip Dinkie."

Five minutes, ten minutes, fifteen minutes passed, and the usual sound of "Oh, pray, massa! Oh, pray, massa!" heard on the occasion of a slave being punished, had not yet proceeded from the barn.

Many of the older negroes gathered around Uncle Ned, for he and Dinkie occupied the same cabin,

and the old, superannuated slave knew more about
the affairs of the conjurer, than anyone else. Ned
told of how, on the previous night, Dinkie had slept
but little, had closely inspected the snake's skin
around his neck, the petrified frog and dried lizard,
in his pockets, and had rubbed himself all over with
goopher; and when he had finished, he knelt, and
exclaimed, —

"Now, good and lovely devil, for more than
twenty years, I have served you faithfully. Before
I got into your service, de white folks bought an'
sold me an' my old wife an' chillen, an' whip me, and
half starve me. Dey did treat me mighty bad, dat
you knows. Den I use to pray to de Lord, but dat
did no good, kase de white folks don't fear de Lord.
But dey fears you, an' ever since I got into your service, I is able to do as I please. No white dares to
lay his hand on me; and dis is all owing to de power
dat you give me. Oh, good and lovely devil! please
to continer dat power. A new oberseer is to come
here to-morrow, an' he wants to get me in his hands.
But, dear devil, I axe you to stand by me in dis my
trial hour, an' I will neber desert you as long as I
live. Continer dis power; make me strong in your
cause; make me to be more faithful to you, an' let
me still be able to conquer my enemies, an' I will
give you all de glory, and will try to deserve a seat
at your right hand."

With bated breath, everyone listened to Uncle
Ned. All had the utmost confidence in Dinkie's
"power." None believed that he would be punished,

while a large number expected to see the roof of the barn burst off at any moment. At last the suspense was broken. The barn door flew open; the overseer and the conjurer came out together, walking side by side, and separated when half-way up the walk. As they parted, Cook went to the field, and Dinkie to his cabin.

The slaves all shook their heads significantly. The fact that the old negro had received no punishment, was evidence of his victory over the slave driver. But how the feat had been accomplished, was a mystery. No one dared to ask Dinkie, for he was always silent, except when he had something to communicate. Everyone was afraid to inquire of the overseer.

There was, however, one faint chance of getting an inkling of what had occurred in the barn, and that was through Uncle Ned. This fact made the old, superannuated slave the hero and centre of attraction, for several days. Many were the applications made to Ned for information, but the old man did not know, or wished to exaggerate the importance of what he had learned.

"I tell you, said Dolly, "Dinkie is a power."

"He's nobody's fool," responded Hannah.

"I would not make him mad wid me, fer dis whole world," ejaculated Jim.

Just then, Nancy, the cook, came in brim full of news. She had given Uncle Ned some "cracklin bread," which had pleased the old man so much that he had opened his bosom, and told her all that he got from Dinkie. This piece of information flew quickly from cabin to cabin, and brought the slaves hastily into the kitchen.

It was night. Nancy sat down, looked around, and told Billy to shut the door. This heightened the interest, so that the fall of a pin could have been heard. All eyes were upon Nancy, and she felt keenly the importance of her position. Her voice was generally loud, with a sharp ring, which could be heard for a long distance, especially in the stillness of the night. But now, Nancy spoke in a whisper, occasionally putting her finger to her mouth, indicating a desire for silence, even when the breathing of those present could be distinctly heard.

"When dey got in de barn, de oberseer said to Dinkie, 'Strip yourself; I don't want to tear your clothes with my whip. I'm going to tear your black skin.'

"Den, you see, Dinkie tole de oberseer to look in de east corner ob de barn. He looked, an' he saw hell, wid all de torments, an' de debble, wid his cloven foot, a-struttin' about dar, jes as ef he was cock ob de walk. An' Dinkie tole Cook, dat ef he lay his his finger on him, he'd call de debble up to take him away."

"An' what did Cook say to dat?" asked Jim.

"Let me 'lone; I didn't tell you all," said Nancy. "Den you see de oberseer turn pale in de face, an' he say to Dinkie, 'Let me go dis time, an' I'll nebber trouble you any more.'"

This concluded Nancy's story, as related to her by old Ned, and religiously believed by all present.

Whatever caused the overseer to change his mind in regard to the flogging of Dinkie, it was certain that he was most thoroughly satisfied to let the old negro off without the threatened punishment; and, although he remained at "Poplar Farm," as overseer, for five years, he never interfered with the conjurer again.

It is not strange that ignorant people should believe in characters of Dinkie's stamp; but it is really marvellous that well-educated men and women should give any countenance whatever, to such delusions as were practised by the oracle of "Poplar Farm."

The following illustration may be taken as a fair sample of the easy manner in which Dinkie carried on his trade.

Miss Martha Lemmy, being on a visit to Mrs. Gaines, took occasion during the day to call upon Dinkie. The conjurer knew the antecedents of his visitor, and was ready to give complete satisfaction in his particular line. When the young lady entered the old man's cabin, he met her, bade her be welcome, and tell what she had come for. She took a seat on one stool, and he on another. Taking the lady's right hand in his, Dinkie spit into its palm, rubbed it, looked at it, shut his one eye, opened it, and said: "I sees a young gentman, an' he's rich, an' owns plenty of land an' a heap o' niggers; an', lo! Miss Marfa, he loves you."

The lady drew a long breath of seeming satisfaction, and asked, "Are you sure that he loves me, Uncle Dinkie?"

"Oh! Miss Marfa, I knows it like a book."

"Have you ever seen the gentleman?" the lady inquired.

The conjurer began rubbing the palm of the snow-white hand, talked to himself in an undertone, smiled, then laughed out, and saying: "Why, Miss Marfa, as I lives it's Mr. Scott, an' he's thinkin' 'bout you now; yes, he's got his mind on you dis bressed minute. But how he's changed sense I seed him de lass time. Now he's got side whiskers an' a mustacher on his chin. But, let me see. Here is somethin' strange. De web looks a little smoky, an' when I gets to dat spot, I can't get along till a little silver is given to me."

Here the lady drew forth her purse and gave the old man a half dollar piece that made his one eye fairly twinkle.

He resumed: "Ah! now de fog is cleared away, an' I see dat Mr. Scott is settin in a rockin-cheer, wid boff feet on de table, an' smokin' a segar."

"Do you think Mr. Scott loves me?" inquired the lady.

"O! yes," responded Dinkie; "he jess sets his whole heart on you. Indeed, Miss Marfa, he's almos' dyin' 'bout you."

"He never told me that he loved me," remarked the lady.

"But den, you see, he's backward, he ain't got his eye-teef cut yet in love matters. But he'll git a little bolder ebbry time he sees you," replied the negro.

"Do you think he'll ever ask me to marry him?"

"O! yes, Miss Marfa, he's sure to do dat. As he sets dar in his rockin-cheer, he looks mighty solemcolly — looks like he wanted to ax you to haf him now."

"Do you think that Mr. Scott likes any other lady, Uncle Dinkie?" asked Miss Lemmy.

"Well, Miss Marfa, I'll jess consult de web an' see." And here the conjurer shut his one eye, opened it, shut it again, talked to himself in an undertone, opened his eye, looked into the lady's hand, and exclaimed: "Ah! Miss Marfa, I see a lady in de way, an' she's got riches; but de web is smoky, an' it needs a little silver to clear it up."

With tears in her eyes, and almost breathless, Miss Lemmy hastily took from her pocket her purse, and handed the old man another piece of money, saying: "Please go on."

Dinkie smiled, shook his head, got up and shut his cabin door, sat down, and again took the lady's hand in his.

"Yes, I see," said he, "I see it's a lady; but bless you soul, Miss Marfa, it's a likeness of you dat Mr. Scott is lookin' at; dat's all."

This morsel of news gave great relief, and Miss Lemmy dried her eyes with joy.

Dinkie then took down the old rusty horseshoe from over his cabin door, held it up, and said: "Dis horseshoe neffer lies." Here he took out of his pocket a bag made of the skin of the rattlesnake, and took from it some goopher, sprinkled it over the horseshoe, saying: "Dis is de stuff, Miss Marfa, dat's

gwine to make you Mr. Scott's conqueror. Long
as you keeps dis goopher 'bout you he can't get

RUNNING DOWN SLAVES WITH DOGS. — Page 82.

away from you; he'll ax you fer a kiss, de berry
next time he meets you, an' he can't help hisself fum

doin' it. No woman can get him fum you so long as you keep dis goopher 'bout you."

Here Dinkie lighted a tallow candle, looked at it, smiled, shook his head, — "You's gwine to marry Mr. Scott in 'bout one year, an' you's gwine to haf thirteen children — sebben boys an' six gals, an' you's gwine to haf a heap of riches."

Just then, Dinkie's interesting revelations were cut short by Ike and Cato bringing along Peter, who, it was said, had been killed by the old bell sheep.

It appears that Peter had a way of playing with the old ram, who was always ready to butt at any one who got in his way. When seeing the ram coming, Peter would get down on his hands and knees and pretend that he was going to have a butting match with the sheep. And when the latter would come full tilt at him, Peter would dodge his head so as to miss the ram, and the latter would jump over the boy, turn around angrily, shake his head and start for another butt at Peter.

This kind of play was repeated sometimes for an hour or more, to the great amusement of both whites and blacks. But, on this occasion, Peter was completely caught. As he was on his hands and knees, the ram started on his usual run for the boy; the latter, in dodging his head, run his face against a stout stub of dry rye stalk, which caused him to quickly jerk up his head, just in time for the sheep to give him a fair butt squarely in the forehead, which knocked Peter senseless. The ram,

elated with his victory, began to back himself for
another lick at Peter, when the men, seeing what
had happened to the poor boy, took him up and
brought him to Dinkie's cabin to be resuscitated, or
"brought to," as they termed it.

Nearly an hour passed in rubbing the boy, before
he began to show signs of consciousness. He "come
to," but he never again accepted a butting match
with the ram.

CHAPTER VIII.

CRUELTY to negroes was not practised in our
section. It is true there were some excep-
tional cases, and some individuals did not take the
care of their servants at all times, that economy
seemed to demand. Yet a certain degree of punishment was actually needed to insure respect to the
master, and good government to the slave population. If a servant disobeyed orders, it was necessary that he should be flogged, to deter others from
following the bad example. If a servant ran away,
he must be caught and brought back, to let the
others see that the same fate awaited them if they
made similar attempts.

While the keeping of bloodhounds, for running
down and catching negroes, was not common, yet a
few were kept by Mr. Tabor, an inferior white man,
near the Corners, who hired them out, or hunted

the runaway, charging so much per day, or a round
sum for the *catch*.

Jerome, a slave owned by the Rev. Mr. Wilson,
when about to be punished by his master, ran away.
Tabor and his dogs were sent for.   The slave-
catcher came, and at once set his dogs upon the
trail.   The parson and some of the neighbors went
along for the fun that was in store.

These dogs will attack a negro, at their master's
bidding, and cling to him as a bull-dog will cling to

TABOR'S CATCH-DOG, "GROWLER."

a beast.   Many are the speculations as to whether
the negro will be secured alive or dead, when these
dogs get on his track.   However, on this occasion,
there was not much danger of ill-treatment, for Mr.
Wilson was a clergyman, and was of a humane turn,
and bargained with Tabor not to injure the slave if
he could help it.

The hunters had been in the wood a short time,
ere they got on the track of two slaves, one of
whom was Jerome.   The negroes immediately bent

their steps toward the swamp, with the hope that the dogs would, when put upon the scent, be unable to follow them through the water. Nearer and nearer the whimpering pack pressed on; their delusion began to dispel.

All at once the truth flashed upon the minds of the fugitives like a glare of light, — that it was Tabor with his dogs! They at last reached the river, and in the negroes plunged, followed by the catch-dog. Jerome was finally caught, and once more in the hands of his master; while the other man found a watery grave. They returned, and the preacher sent his slave to the city jail for safe-keeping.

While the planters would employ Tabor, without hesitation, to hunt down their negroes, they would not receive him into their houses as a visitor any sooner than they would one of their own slaves. Tabor was, however, considered one of the better class of poor whites, a number of whom had a religious society in that neighborhood. The pastor of the poor whites was the Rev. Martin Louder, somewhat of a genius in his own way. The following sermon, preached by him, about the time of which I write, will well illustrate the character of the people for whom he labored.

More than two long, weary hours had now elapsed since the audience had been convened, and the people began to exhibit slight signs of fatigue. Some few scrapings and rasping of cowhide boots on the floor, an audible yawn or two, a little twisting and turning on the narrow, uncomfortable seats, while, in one or two instances, a somnolent soul or two snored outright. These palpable signs were not lost upon our old friend Louder. He cast an eye (emphatically, an eye) over the assemblage, and then — he spoke : —

"My dear breethering, and beloved sistering ! You've ben a long time a settin' on your seats. You're tired, I know, an' I don't expect you want to hear the ole daddy preach. Ef you don't want to hear the ole man, jist give him the least bit of a sign. Cough. Hold up your hand. Ennything, an' Louder'll sit rite down. He'll dry up in a minit."

At this juncture of affairs, Louder paused for a reply. He glanced furtively over the audience, in search of the individual who might be "tired of settin' on his seat," but no sign was made : no such malcontent came within the visual range.

"Go on, Brother Louder ! " said a sonorous voice in the " amen corner " of the house. Thus encouraged, the speaker proceeded in his remarks : —

"Well, then, breethering, sense you say so, Louder'll perceed ; but he don't intend to preach a reg'lar sermon, for it's a gittin' late, and our sect which hit don't believe in eatin' cold vittles on the Lord's day. My breethering, ef the ole Louder gits outen the rite track, I want you to call him back. He don't want to teach you any error. He don't want' to preach nuthin' but what's found between the leds of this blessed Book."

"My dear breethering, the Lord raised up his servant, Moses, that he should fetch his people Isrel up outen that wicked land — ah. Then Moses, he went out from the face of the Lord, and departed hence unto the courts of the old tyranickle king — ah. An' what sez you, Moses? Ah, sez he, Moses sez, sez he to that wicked old Faro: Thus sez the Lord God of hosts, sez he: Let my Isrel go — ah. An' what sez the ole, hard-hearted king — ah? Ah! sez Faro, sez he, who is the Lord God of hosts, sez he, that I should obey his voice — ah? An' now what sez you, Moses — ah. Ah, Moses sez, sez he: Thus saith the Lord God of Isrel, let my people go, that they mought worship me, sez the Lord, in the wilderness — ah. But — ah! my beloved breethering an' my harden', impenitent frien's — ah, did the ole, hard-hearted king harken to the words of Moses, and let my people go — ah? Nary time."

This last remark, made in an ordinary, conversational tone of voice, was so sudden and unexpected that the change, the transition from the singing state was electrical.

"An' then, my beloved breethering an' sistering, what next — ah? What sez you, Moses, to Faro — that contrary ole king — ah? Ah, Moses sez to Faro, sez he, Moses sez, sez he: Thus seth the Lord God of Isrel: Let my people go, sez the Lord, leest I come, sez he, and smite you with a cuss — ah! An' what sez Faro, the ole tyranickle king — ah? Ah, sez he, sez ole Faro, Let their tasks be doubled, and leest they mought grumble, sez he, those bricks shall be made without straw — ah!   [Vox naturale.] Made 'em pluck up grass an' stubble outen the fields, breethering, to mix with their mud.   Mity hard on the pore critters; warn't it, Brother Flood Gate?" [The individual thus interrogated replied, "Jess so;" and "ole Louder" moved along.]

"An' what next — ah?   Did the ole king let my people Isrel go — ah?   No, my dear breethering, he retched out his pizen hand, and he hilt 'em fash — ah.   Then the Lord was wroth with that wicked ole king — ah.   An' the Lord, he sed to Moses, sez he: Moses, stretch forth now thy rod over the rivers an' the ponds of this wicked land — ah; an' behold, sez he, when thou stretch out thy rod, sez the Lord, all the waters shall be turned into blood — ah!   Then Moses, he tuck his rod, an' he done as the Lord God of Isrel had commanded his servant Moses to do — ah.   An' what then, say you, my breethering — ah? Why, lo an' behold! the rivers of that wicked land was all turned into blood — ah; an' all the fish an' all the frogs in them streams an' waters died a—h!"

"Yes!" said the speaker, lowering his voice to a natural tone, and glancing out of the open window at the dry and dusty road, for we were at the time suffering from a protracted drouth: "An' I believe the frogs will all die now, unless we get some rain purty soon.   What do you think about it, Brother Waters?"   [This interrogatory was addressed to a fine, portly-looking old man in the congregation. Brother W. nodded assent, and old Louder resumed the thread of his discourse.] "Ah, my beloved breethering, that was a hard time on old Faro an' his wicked crowd — ah. For the waters was loath-

REV. MR. WILSON AND HIS CAPTURED SLAVE. — Page 83.

some to the people, an' it smelt so bad none of 'em cood drink it; an' what next — ah? Did the ole king obey the voice of the Lord, and let my people Isrel go — ah? Ah, no, my breethering, not by a long sight — ah. For he hilt out agin the Lord, and obeyed not his voice — ah. Then the Lord sent a gang of bull-frogs into that wicked land — ah. An' they went hoppin' an' lopin' about all over the country, into the vittles, an' everywhere else — ah. My breethering, the old Louder thinks that was a des'-prit time — ah. But all woodent do — ah. Ole Faro was as stubborn as one of Louder's mules — ah, an' he woodent let the chosen seed go up outen the land of bondage — ah. Then the Lord sent a mighty hail, an', arter that, his devourin' locuses — ah! An' they et up blamed nigh everything on the face of the eth—ah."

"Let not yore harts be trubbled, for the truth is mitay and must prevale — ah. Brother Creek, you don't seem to be doin' much of ennything, suppose you raise a tune!"

This remark was addressed to a tall, lank, hollow-jawed old man, in the congregation, with a great shock of "grizzled gray" hair.

"Wait a minit, Brother Louder, till I git on my glasses!" was the reply of Brother Creek, who proceeded to draw from his pocket an oblong tin case, which opened and shut with a tremendous snap, from which he drew a pair of iron-rimmed spectacles. These he carefully "dusted" with his handkerchief, and then turned to the hymn which the preacher had selected and read out to the congregation. After considerable deliberation, and some

clearing of the throat, hawking, spitting, etc., and
other preliminaries, Brother Creek, in a quavering,
split sort of voice, opened out on the tune.

Louder seemed uneasy. It was evident that he
feared a failure on the part of the worthy brother.
At the end of the first line, he exclaimed : —

"'Pears to me, Brother Creek, you hain't got the
right miter."

Brother Creek suspended operations a moment,
and replied, "I am purty kerrect, ginerally, Brother
Louder, an' I'm confident she'll come out all right!"

"Well," said Louder, "we'll try her agin," and
the choral strain, under the supervision of Brother
Creek, was resumed in the following words : —

> " When I was a mourner just like you,
>   Washed in the blood of the Lamb,
>   I fasted and prayed till I got through,
>   Washed in the blood of the Lamb.

CHORUS. — " Come along, sinner, and go with us ;
>   If you don't you will be cussed.

> " Religion's like a blooming rose,
>   Washed in the blood of the Lamb,
>   As none but those that feel it knows,
>   Washed in the blood of the Lamb." — *Cho.*

The singing, joined in by all present, brought the
enthusiasm of the assembly up to white heat, and
the shouting, with the loud " Amen," " God save the
sinner," " Sing it, brother, sing it," made the welkin
ring.

CHAPTER IX.

WHILE the "peculiar institution" was a great injury to both master and slaves, yet there was considerable truth in the oft-repeated saying that the slave "was happy." It was indeed, a low kind of happiness, existing only where masters were disposed to treat their servants kindly, and where the proverbial light-heartedness of the latter prevailed. History shows that of all races, the African was best adapted to be the "hewers of wood, and drawers of water."

Sympathetic in his nature, thoughtless in his feelings, both alimentativeness and amativeness large, the negro is better adapted to follow than to lead. His wants easily supplied, generous to a fault, large fund of humor, brimful of music, he has ever been found the best and most accommodating of servants. The slave would often get rid of punishment by his wit; and even when being flogged, the master's heart has been moved to pity, by the humorous appeals of his victim. House servants in the cities and villages, and even on plantations, were considered privileged classes. Nevertheless, the field hands were not without their happy hours.

An old-fashioned corn-shucking took place once a year, on "Poplar Farm," which afforded pleasant amusement for the out-door negroes for miles around. On these occasions, the servants, on all plantations, were allowed to attend by mere invitation of the blacks where the corn was to be shucked.

As the grain was brought in from the field, it was left in a pile near the corn-cribs. The night appointed, and invitations sent out, slaves from plantations five or six miles away, would assemble and join on the road, and in large bodies march along, singing their melodious plantation songs.

To hear three or four of these gangs coming from different directions, their leaders giving out the words, and the whole company joining in the chorus, would indeed surpass anything ever produced by "Haverly's Ministrels," and many of their jokes and witticisms were never equalled by Sam Lucas or Billy Kersands.

A supper was always supplied by the planter on whose farm the shucking was to take place. Often when approaching the place, the singers would speculate on what they were going to have for supper. The following song was frequently sung : —

> " All dem puty gals will be dar,
>   Shuck dat corn before you eat.
> Dey will fix it fer us rare,
>   Shuck dat corn before you eat.
> I know dat supper will be big,
>   Shuck dat corn before you eat.
> I think I smell a fine roast pig,
>   Shuck dat corn before you eat.
> A supper is provided, so dey said,
>   Shuck dat corn before you eat.
> I hope dey'll have some nice wheat bread,
>   Shuck dat corn before you eat.
> I hope dey'll have some coffee dar,
>   Shuck dat corn before you eat.

I hope dey'll have some whisky dar,
    Shuck dat corn before you eat.
I think I'll fill my pockets full,
    Shuck dat corn before you eat.
Stuff dat coon an' bake him down,
    Shuck dat corn before you eat.
I speck some niggers dar from town,
    Shuck dat corn before you eat.
Please cook dat turkey nice an' brown.
    Shuck dat corn before you eat.
By de side of dat turkey I'll be foun,
    Shuck dat corn before you eat.
I smell de supper, dat I do,
    Shuck dat corn before you eat.
On de table will be a stew,
    Shuck dat corn, etc."

Burning pine knots, held by some of the boys,
usually furnished light for the occasion. Two hours
is generally sufficient time to finish up a large shucking; where five hundred bushels of corn is thrown
into the cribs as the shuck is taken off. The
work is made comparatively light by the singing,
which never ceases till they go to the supper table.
Something like the following is sung during the
evening:

" De possum meat am good to eat,
    Carve him to de heart;
You'll always find him good and sweet,
    Carve him to de heart;
My dog did bark, and I went to see,
    Carve him to de heart;
And dar was a possum up dat tree,
    Carve him to de heart.

CHORUS. — " Carve dat possum, carve dat possum children,
   Carve dat possum, carve him to de heart;
  Oh, carve dat possum, carve dat possum chil-
    dren,
   Carve dat possum, carve him to de heart.

 " I reached up for to pull him in,
  Carve him to de heart;
 De possum he began to grin,
  Carve him to de heart;
 I carried him home and dressed him off,
  Carve him to de heart;
 I hung him dat night in de frost,
  Carve him to de heart.
CHORUS. — " Carve dat possum, etc.

 " De way to cook de possum sound,
  Carve him to de heart;
 Fust par-bile him, den bake him brown,
  Carve him to de heart;
 Lay sweet potatoes in de pan,
  Carve him to de heart;
 De sweetest eatin' in de lan,'
  Carve him to de heart.
CHORUS. — " Carve dat possum, etc."

Should a poor supper be furnished, on such an occasion, you would hear remarks from all parts of the table, —

" Take dat rose pig 'way from dis table."

" What rose pig? you see any rose pig here?"

" Ha, ha, ha! Dis ain't de place to see rose pig."

" Pass up some dat turkey wid clam sauce."

"Don't talk about dat turkey; he was gone afore we come."

"Dis is de las' time I shucks corn at dis farm."

"Dis is a cheap farm, cheap owner, an' a cheap supper."

"He's talkin' it, ain't he?"

"Dis is de tuffest meat dat I is been called upon to eat fer many a day; you's got to have teeth sharp as a saw to eat dis meat."

"Spose you ain't got no teef, den what you gwine to do?"

"Why, ef you ain't got no teef you muss *gum it!*"

"Ha, ha, ha!" from the whole company, was heard.

On leaving the corn-shucking farm, each gang of men, headed by their leader, would sing during the entire journey home. Some few, however, having their dogs with them, would start on the trail of a coon, possum, or some other game, which might keep them out till nearly morning.

To the Christmas holidays, the slaves were greatly indebted for winter recreation; for long custom had given to them the whole week from Christmas day to the coming in of the New Year.

On "Poplar Farm," the hands drew their share of clothing on Christmas day for the year. The clothing for both men and women was made up by women kept for general sewing and housework. One pair of pants, and two shirts, made the entire stock for a male field hand.

The women's garments were manufactured from the same goods that the men received. Many of the men worked at night for themselves, making splint and corn brooms, baskets, shuck mats, and axe-handles, which they would sell in the city during Christmas week. Each slave was furnished with a pass, something like the following : —

" Please let my boy, Jim, pass anywhere in this county, until Jan. 1, 1834, *and oblige*   *Respectfully,*
　　　　　　　" JOHN GAINES, M.D.
　　　　　" ' Poplar Farm,' St. Louis County, Mo."

With the above precious document in his pocket, a load of baskets, brooms, mats, and axe-handles on his back, a bag hanging across his shoulders, with a jug in each end, — one for the whiskey, and the other for the molasses, — the slaves trudged off to town at night, singing, —

　　　" Hurra, for good ole massa,
　　　　　He give me de pass to go to de city.
　　　Hurra, for good ole missis,
　　　　　She bile de pot, and giv me de licker.
　　　　　　　Hurra, I'm goin to de city."

　　　" When de sun rise in de mornin',
　　　　　Jes' above de yaller corn,
　　　You'll fin' dis nigger has take warnin',
　　　　　An's gone when de driver blows his horn.

　　　" Hurra, for good ole massa,
　　　　　He giv me de pass to go to de city.
　　　Hurra for good ole missis,
　　　　　She bile de pot, and give me de licker.
　　　　　　　Hurra, I'm goin to de city."

Both the Methodists and Baptists, — the religious denominations to which the blacks generally belong, — never fail to be in the midst of a revival meeting during the holidays, and most of the slaves from the country hasten to these gatherings. Some, however, spend their time at the dances, raffles, cock-fights, foot-races, and other amusements that present themselves.

CHAPTER X

A YOUNG and beautiful lady, closely veiled and attired in black, arrived one morning at "Poplar Farm," and was shown immediately into a room in the eastern wing, where she remained, attended only by old Nancy. That the lady belonged to the better class was evident from her dress, refined manners, and the inviolable secrecy of her stay at the residence of Dr. Gaines. At last the lady gave birth to a child, which was placed under the care of Isabella, a quadroon servant, who had recently lost a baby of her own.

The lady left the premises as mysteriously as she had come, and nothing more was ever seen or heard of her, certainly not by the negroes. The child, which was evidently of pure Anglo-Saxon blood, was called Lola, and grew up amongst the negro children of the place, to be a bright, pretty girl, to whom her adopted mother seemed very much at-

more old rip-off

tached. At the time of which I write, Lola was
eight years old, and her presence on the plantation
began to annoy the white members of Dr. Gaines'
family, especially when strangers visited the place.

The appearance of Mr. Walker, the noted slave
speculator, on the plantation, and whom it was said,
had been sent for, created no little excitement
amongst the slaves; and great was the surprise to
the blacks, when they saw the trader taking Isabella
and Lola with him at his departure. Unable to sell
the little white girl at any price, Mr. Walker gave
her to Mr. George Savage, who having no children
of his own adopted the child.

Isabella was sold to a gentleman, who took her
to Washington. The grief of the quadroon at being
separated from her adopted child was intense, and
greatly annoyed her new master, who determined to
sell her on his arrival home. Isabella was sold to
the slave-trader, Jennings, who placed the woman
in one of the private slave-pens, or prisons, a number of which then disgraced the national capital.

Jennings intended to send Isabella to the New
Orleans market, as soon as he purchased a sufficient
number. At the dusk of the evening, previous to
the day she was to be sent off, as the old prison was
being closed for the night, Isabella suddenly darted
past the keeper, and ran for her life. It was not a
great distance from the prison to the long bridge
which passes from the lower part of the city, across
the Potomac to the extensive forests and woodlands
of the celebrated Arlington Heights, then occupied

by that distinguished relative and descendant of the
immortal Washington, Mr. Geo. W. Custis. Thither
the poor fugitive directed her flight. So unexpected
was her escape, that she had gained several rods
the start before the keeper had secured the other
prisoners, and rallied his assistants to aid in the
pursuit. It was at an hour, and in a part of the
city where horses could not easily be obtained for
the chase; no bloodhounds were at hand to run
down the flying woman, and for once it seemed as
if there was to be a fair trial of speed and endur-
ance between the slave and the slave-catchers.

The keeper and his force raised the hue-and-cry
on her path as they followed close behind; but so
rapid was the flight along the wide avenue, that the
astonished citizens, as they poured forth from their
dwellings to learn the cause of alarm, were only able
to comprehend the nature of the case in time to fall
in with the motley throng in pursuit, or raise an
anxious prayer to heaven, as they refused to join in
the chase (as many a one did that night), that the
panting fugitive might escape, and the merciless
soul-dealer for once be disappointed of his prey.
And now, with the speed of an arrow, having passed
the avenue, with the distance between her and her
pursuers constantly increasing, this poor, hunted
female gained the "Long Bridge," as it is called,
where interruption seemed improbable. Already
her heart began to beat high with the hope of success. She had only to pass three-quarters of a mile
across the bridge, when she could bury herself in a

vast forest, just at the time when the curtain of
night would close around her, and protect her from
the pursuit of her enemies.

But God, by His providence, had otherwise determined. He had ordained that an appalling tragedy
should be enacted that night within plain sight of
the President's house, and the Capitol of the Union,
which would be an evidence, wherever it should be
known, of the unconquerable love of liberty which
the human heart may inherit, as well as a fresh
admonition to the slave-dealer of the cruelty and
enormity of his crimes.

Just as the pursuers passed the high draw, soon
after entering upon the bridge, they beheld three
men slowly approaching from the Virginia side.
They immediately called to them to arrest the fugitive, proclaiming her a runaway slave. True to
their Virginia instincts, as she came near, they
formed a line across the narrow bridge to intercept
her. Seeing that escape was impossible in that
quarter, she stopped suddenly, and turned upon her
pursuers.

On came the profane and ribald gang, faster than
ever, already exulting in her capture, and threatening punishment for her flight. For a moment, she
looked wildly and anxiously around to see if there
was no hope of escape, on either hand; far down
below, rolled the deep, foaming waters of the
Potomac, and before and behind were the rapidly
approaching steps and noisy voices of her pursuers.

Seeing how vain would be any further effort to

escape, her resolution was instantly taken. She clasped her hands convulsively together, raised her tearful and imploring eyes towards heaven, and begged for the mercy and compassion there, which was unjustly denied her on earth; then, with a single bound, vaulted over the railing of the bridge, and sank forever beneath the angry and foaming waters of the river.

In the meantime Mr. and Mrs. Savage were becoming more and more interested in the child, Lola, whom they had adopted, and who was fast developing into an intellectual and beautiful girl, whose bright, sparkling hazel eyes, snow-white teeth and alabaster complexion caused her to be admired by all. In time, Lola become highly educated, and was duly introduced into the best society.

The cholera of 1832, in its ravages, swept off many of St. Louis' most valued citizens, and among them, Mr. George Savage. Mrs. Savage, who was then in ill-health, regarded Lola with even greater solicitude, than during the lifetime of her late husband. Lola had been amply provided for by Mr. Savage, in his will. She was being courted by Mr. Martin Phelps, previous to the death of her adopted father, and the failing health of Mrs. Savage hastened the nuptials.

The marriage of Mr. Phelps and Miss Savage partook more of a private than of a public affair, owing to the recent death of Mr. Savage. Mr. Phelps' residence was at the outskirts of the city, in the vicinity of what was known as the "Mound," and

was a lovely spot.   The lady had brought considerable property to her husband.

One morning in the month of December, and only
about three months after the marriage of the Phelps's,
two men alighted from a carriage, at Mr. Phelps'
door, rang the bell, and were admitted by the servant.   Mr. Phelps hastened from the breakfast-table,
as the servant informed him of the presence of the
strangers.

On entering the sitting-room, the host recognized
one of the men as Officer Mull, while the other
announced himself as James Walker, and said, —

"I have come, Mr. Phelps, on rather an unpleasant errand.   You've got a slave in your house that
belongs to me."

"I think you are mistaken, sir," replied Mr.
Phelps; "my servants are all hired from Major
Ben. O'Fallon."

Walker put on a sinister smile, and blandly continued, "I see, sir, that you don't understand me.
Ten years ago I bought a slave child from Dr.
Gaines, and lent her to Mr. George Savage, and I
understand she's in your employ, and I've come to
get her," and here the slave speculator took from
his side pocket a large sheepskin pocket book, and
drew forth the identical bill of sale of Lola, given
to him by Dr. Gaines at the time of the selling of
Isabella and the child.

"Good heavens!" exclaimed Mr. Phelps, "that
paper, if it means anything, it means my wife."

"I can't help what it means," remarked Walker;

"here's the bill of sale, and here's the officer to get me my nigger."

"There must be a mistake here. It is true that my wife was the adopted daughter of the late Mr. George Savage, but there is not a drop of negro blood in her veins; and I doubt, sir, if you have ever seen her."

"Well, sir," said Walker, "jest bring her in the room, and I guess she'll know me."

Feeling confident that the bill of sale had no reference to his wife, Mr. Phelps rang the bell, and told the boy that answered it to ask his mistress to come in. A moment or two later, and the lady entered the room.

"My dear," said Mr. Phelps, "are you acquainted with either of these gentlemen?"

The lady looked, hesitated, and replied, "I think not."

Then Walker arose, stepped towards the window, where he could be seen to better advantage, and said, "Why, Lola, have you forgotten me, its only about ten years since I brought you from 'Poplar Farm,' and lent you to Mr. Savage. Ha, ha, ha!"

This coarse laugh of the rough, uneducated negro-trader had not ceased, when Lola gave a heart-rending shriek, and fell fainting upon the floor.

"I thought she'd know me when I jogged her memory," said Walker, as he re-seated himself.

Mr. Phelps sprang to his wife, and lifted her from the floor, and placed her upon the sofa.

"Throw a little of Adam's ale in her face, and

that'll bring her to. I've seen 'em faint afore; but they allers come to," said the trader.

LEAP OF THE FUGITIVE SLAVE.

"I thank you, sir, but I will attend to my own affairs," said Mr. Phelps, in a rather petulant tone.

"Yes," replied Walker; "but she's mine, and I want to see that she comes to."

As soon as she revived, Mr. Phelps led his wife from the room. A conference of an hour took place on the return of Mr. Phelps to the parlor, which closed with the understanding that a legal examination of the papers should settle the whole question the next day.

At the appointed time, on the following morning, one of the ablest lawyers in the city, Col. Strawther, pronounced the bill of sale genuine, for it had been drawn up by Justice McGuyer, and witnessed by George Kennelly and Wilson P. Hunt.

For this claim, Walker expressed a willingness to sell the woman for two thousand dollars. The payment of the money would have been a small matter, if it had not carried with it the proof that Lola was a slave, which was undeniable evidence that she had negro blood in her veins.

Yet such was the result, for Dr. Gaines had been dead these three years, and whoever Lola's mother was, even if living, she would not come forth to vindicate the free birth of her child.

Mr. Phelps was a man of fine sensibility and was affectionately attached to his wife. However, it was a grave question to be settled in his mind, whether his honor as a Southern gentleman, and his standing in society would allow him to acknowledge a woman as his wife, in whose veins coursed the accursed blood of the negro slave.

Long was the struggle between love and duty,

but the shame of public gaze and the ostracism of
society decided the matter in favor of duty, and the
young and lovely wife was informed by the husband
that they must separate, never to meet again.   In-
describable were the feelings of Lola, as she begged
him, upon her knees, not to leave her.   The room
was horrible in its darkness, — her mind lost its
reasoning powers for a time.   At last consciousness
returned, but only to awaken in her the loneliness
of her condition, and the unfriendliness of that law
and society that dooms one to everlasting disgrace
for a blood taint, which the victim did not have.

Ten days after the proving of the bill of sale, the
innocent Lola died of a broken heart, and was interred in the negro burial ground, with not a white
face to follow the corpse to its last resting-place.
Such is American race prejudice.

CHAPTER XI.

THE invention of the Whitney cotton gin, nearly
fifty years ago, created a wonderful rise in the
price of slaves in the cotton States.   The value of
able-bodied men, fit for field-hands, advanced from
five hundred to twelve hundred dollars, in the short
space of five years.   In 1850, a prime field-hand
was worth two thousand dollars.   The price of
women rose in proportion; they being valued at

about three hundred dollars less each than the men. This change in the price of slaves caused a lucrative business to spring up, both in the breeding of slaves and the sending of them to the States needing their services. Virginia, Kentucky, Missouri, Tennessee, and North Carolina became the slave-raising sections; Virginia, however, was always considered the banner State. To the traffic in human beings, more than to any other of its evils, is the institution indebted for its overthrow.

From the picture on the heading of *The Liberator*, down to the smallest tract printed against slavery, the separation of families was the chief object of those exposing the great American sin. The tearing asunder of husbands and wives, of parents and children, and the gangs of men and women chained together, *en route* for the New-Orleans' market, furnished newspaper correspondents with items that never wanted readers. These newspaper paragraphs were not unfrequently made stronger by the fact that many of the slaves were as white as those who offered them for sale, and the close resemblance of the victim to the trader, often reminded the purchaser that the same blood coursed through the veins of both.

The removal of Dr. Gaines from "Poplar Farm" to St. Louis, gave me an opportunity of seeing the worst features of the internal slave-trade. For many years Missouri drove a brisk business in the selling of her sons and daughters, the greater number of whom passed through the city of St. Louis.

For a long time, James Walker was the principal
speculator in this species of property. The early
life of this man had been spent as a drayman, first
working for others, then for himself, and eventually
purchasing men who worked with him. At last,
disposing of his horses and drays, he took his faithful men to the Louisiana market and sold them.
This was the commencement of a career of cruelty,
that, in all probability, had no equal in the annals
of the American slave trade.

A more repulsive-looking person could scarcely
be found in any community of bad-looking men
than Walker. Tall, lean, and lank, with high
cheek-bones, face much pitted with the small-pox,
gray eyes, with red eyebrows, and sandy whiskers,
he indeed stood alone without mate or fellow in
looks. He prided himself upon what he called his
goodness of heart, and was always speaking of his
humanity.

Walker often boasted that he never separated
families if he could " persuade the purchaser to take
the whole lot." He would always advertise in the
New Orleans' papers that he would be there with a
prime lot of able-bodied slaves, men and women,
fit for field-service, with a few extra ones calculated
for house servants, — all between the ages of fifteen
and twenty-five years ; but like most men who make
a business of speculating in human beings, he often
bought many who were far advanced in years, and
would try to pass them off for five or six years
younger than they were. Few persons can arrive

at anything approaching the real age of the negro,
by mere observation, unless they are well acquainted
with the race.   Therefore, the slave-trader frequently
carried out the deception with perfect impunity.

As soon as the steamer would leave the wharf, and
was fairly on the bosom of the broad Mississippi,
the speculator would call his servant Pompey to
him, and instruct him as to getting the slaves ready
for the market. If any of the blacks looked as
if they were older than they were advertised to be,
it was Pompey's business to fit them for the day of
sale.

Pomp, as he was usually called by the trader, was
of real negro blood, and would often say, when
alluding to himself, "Dis nigger am no counterfeit,
he is de ginuine artikle.   Dis chile is none of your
haf-and-haf, dere is no bogus about him."

Pompey was of low stature, round face, and, like
most of his race, had a set of teeth, which, for
whiteness and beauty, could not be surpassed; his
eyes were large, lips thick, and hair short and
woolly.   Pomp had been with Walker so long, and
seen so much of buying and selling of his fellow-
creatures, that he appeared perfectly indifferent to
the heart-rending scenes which daily occurred in his
presence.   Such is the force of habit: —

> " Vice is a monster of such frightful mien,
>   That to be hated, needs but to be seen;
>   But seen too oft, familiar with its face,
>   We first endure, then pity, then embrace."

Before reaching the place of destination, Pompey would pick out the older portion and say, "I is de chap dat is to get you ready for de Orleans market, so dat you will bring marser a good price. How old is you?" addressing himself to a man that showed some age.

"Ef I live to see next corn-plantin' time, I'll be forty."

"Dat may be," replied Pompey, "but now you is only thirty years old; dat's what marser says you is to be."

"I know I is mo' dan dat," responded the man.

"I can't help nuffin' 'bout dat," returned Pompey; "but when you get in de market, an' any one ax you how old you is, an' you tell um you is forty, massa will tie you up, an' when he is done whippin' you, you'll be glad to say you's only thirty."

"Well den, I reckon I is only thirty," said the slave.

"What is your name?" asked Pompey of another man in the group.

"Jeems," was the response.

"Oh! Uncle Jim, is it?"

"Yes."

"Den you muss' hab all dem gray whiskers shaved off, and dem gray hairs plucked out of your head. De fack is, you's got ole too quick." This was all said by Pompey in a manner which showed that he knew his business.

"How ole is you?" asked Pompey of a tall, strong-looking man.

"I am twenty-nine, nex' Christmas Eve," said the man.

"What's your name?"

"My name is Tobias," replied the slave.

"Tobias!" ejaculated Pompey, with a sneer, that told that he was ready to show his brief authority. "Now you's puttin' on airs. Your name is Toby, an' why can't you tell the truf? Remember, now, dat you is twenty-three years ole; an' afore you goes in de market your face muss' be greased; fer I see you's one of dem kind o' ashy niggers, an' a little grease will make your face look black an' slick, an' make you look younger."

Pompey reported to his master the condition of affairs, when the latter said, "Be sure that the niggers don't forget what you have taught them, for our luck depends a great deal upon the appearance of our stock."

With this lot of slaves was a beautiful quadroon, a girl of twenty years, fair as most white women, with hair a little wavy, large black eyes, and a countenance that betokened intelligence beyond the common house servant. Her name was Marion, and the jealousy of the mistress, so common in those days, was the cause of her being sold.

Not far from Canal Street, in the city of New Orleans, in the old days of slavery, stood a two-story, flat building, surrounded by a stone wall, some twelve feet high, the top of which was covered with bits of glass, and so constructed as to prevent even the possibility of any one's passing over it without sustaining great injury. Many of the rooms in this building resembled the cells of a prison, and in a small apartment, near the "office," were to be seen any number of iron collars, hobbles, hand-cuffs, thumb-screws, cowhides, chains, gags, and yokes.

A back-yard, enclosed by a high wall, looked like the play-ground attached to one of our large New England schools, in which were rows of benches and swings. Attached to the back premises was a good-sized kitchen, where, at the time of which we write, two old negresses were at work, stewing, boiling, and baking, and occasionally wiping the perspiration from their furrowed and swarthy brows.

The slave-trader, Walker, on his arrival at New Orleans, took up his quarters here, with his gang of human cattle, and the morning after, at ten o'clock, they were exhibited for sale. First of all, came the beautiful Marion, whose pale countenance and dejected look, told how many sad hours she had passed since parting with her mother. There, too, was a poor woman, who had been separated from her husband, and another woman, whose looks and manners were expressive of deep anguish, sat by her side. There was "Uncle Jeems," with his whiskers off, his face shaven clean, and the gray hairs plucked out, ready to be sold for ten years younger than he was. Toby was also there, with his face shaven and greased, ready for inspection.

The examination commenced, and was carried on in

such a manner as to shock the feelings of any one not entirely devoid of the milk of human kindness.

"What are you wiping your eyes for?" inquired a fat, red-faced man, with a white hat set on one side of his head and a cigar in his mouth, of a woman who sat on one of the benches.

"Because I left my man behind."

"Oh, if I buy you, I will furnish you with a better man than you left. I've got lots of young bucks on my farm," responded the man.

"I don't want and never will have another man," replied the woman.

"What's your name?" asked a man, in a straw hat, of a tall negro, who stood with his arms folded across his breast, leaning against the wall.

"My name is Aaron, sar."

"How old are you?"

"Twenty-five."

"Where were you raised?"

"In ole Virginny, sar."

"How many men have owned you?"

"Four."

"Do you enjoy good health?"

"Yes, sar."

"How long did you live with your first owner?"

"Twenty years."

"Did you ever run away?"

"No, sar."

"Did you ever strike your master?"

"No sar."

"Were you ever whipped much?"

" No, sar; I spose I didn't desarve it, sar."

" How long did you live with your second master? "

" Ten years, sar."

" Have you a good appetite? "

" Yes, sar."

" Can you eat your allowance? "

" Yes, sar, — when I can get it."

" Where were you employed in Virginia? "

" I worked in de tobacker fiel'."

" In the tobacco field, eh? "

" Yes, sar."

" How old did you say you was? "

" Twenty-five, sar, nex' sweet-'tater-diggin' time."

" I am a cotton-planter, and if I buy you, you will have to work in the cotton field.   My men pick one hundred and fifty pounds a day, and the women one hundred and forty pounds; and those who fail to perform their task receive five stripes for each pound that is wanting.   Now do you think you could keep up with the rest of the hands? "

" I don't know, sar, but I reckon I'd have to."

" How long did you live with your third master? "

" Three years, sar," replied the slave.

" Why, that makes you thirty-three; I thought you told me you were only twenty-five."

Aaron now looked first at the planter, then at the trader, and seemed perfectly bewildered.   He had forgotten the lesson given him by Pompey, relative to his age; and the planter's circuitous questions — doubtless to find out the slave's real age — had thrown the negro off his guard.

"I must see your back, so as to know how much you have been whipped, before I think of buying."

Pompey, who had been standing by during the examination, thought that his services were now required, and, stepping forth with a degree of officiousness, said to Aaron: — "Don't you hear de gemman tell you he wants to zamin you? Cum, unharness yo-seff, ole boy, an' don't be standin' dar."

Aaron was examined, and pronounced "sound"; yet the conflicting statement about his age was not satisfactory.

On the following trip down the river, Walker halted at Vicksburg, with a "prime lot of slaves," and a circumstance occurred which shows what the slaves in those days would resort to, to save themselves from flogging, while, at the same time, it exhibits the quick wit of the race.

While entertaining some of his purchasers at the hotel, Walker ordered Pompey to hand the wine around to his guests. In doing this, the servant upset a glass of wine upon a gentleman's lap. For this mishap, the trader determined to have his servant punished. He, therefore, gave Pompey a sealed note, and ordered him to take it to the slave prison. The servant, suspecting that all was not right, hastened to open the note before the wafer had dried; and passing the steamboat landing, he got a sailor to read the note, which proved to be, as Pompey had suspected, an order to have him receive "thirty-nine stripes upon the bare back."

Walker had given the man a silver dollar, with orders to deliver it, with the note, to the jailor, for it was common in those days for persons who wanted their servants punished and did not wish to do it themselves, to send them to the "slave pen," and have it done; the price for which was one dollar.

How to escape the flogging, and yet bring back

WALKER, THE SLAVE TRADER.

to his master the evidence of having been punished, perplexed the fertile brain of Pompey. However, the servant was equal to the occasion. Standing in front of the "slave pen," the negro saw another well dressed colored man coming up the street, and he determined to inquire in regard to how they did the whipping there.

"How de do, sar," said Pompey, addressing the colored brother. "Do you live here?"

"Oh! no," replied the stranger, "I am a free man, and belong in Pittsburgh, Pa."

"Ah! ha, den you don't live here," said Pompey.

"No, I left my boat here last week, and I have been trying every day to get something to do. I'm pretty well out of money, and I'd do almost anything just now."

A thought flashed upon Pompey's mind — this was his occasion.

"Well," said the slave, "ef you want a job, whar you can make some money quick, I specks I can help you."

"If you will," replied the free man, you'll do me a great favor."

"Here, then," said Pompey, "take dis note, an' go in to dat prison, dar, an' dey will give you a trunk, bring it out, an' I'll tell you where to carry it to, an' here's a dollar; dat will pay you, won't it?"

"Yes," replied the man, with many thanks; and taking the note and the shining coin, with smiles, he went to the "Bell Gate," and gave the bell a loud ring. The gate flew open, and in he went.

The man had scarcely disappeared, ere Pompey had crossed the street, and was standing at the gate, listening to the conversation then going on between the jailor and the free colored man.

"Where is the dollar that you got with this note?" asked the "*whipper*," as he finished reading the epistle.

"Here it is, sir; he gave it to me," said the man, with no little surprise.

"Hand it here," responded the jailor, in a rough voice. "There, now; take this nigger, Pete, and strap him down upon the stretcher, and get him ready for business."

"What are you going to do to me!" cried the horrified man, at the jailor's announcement.

"You'll know, damn quick!" was the response.

The resistance of the innocent man caused the "whipper" to call in three other sturdy blacks, and, in a few minutes, the victim was fastened upon the stretcher, face downwards, his clothing removed, and the strong-armed white negro-whipper standing over him with uplifted whip.

The cries and groans of the poor man, as the heavy instrument of torture fell upon his bare back, aroused Pompey, who retreated across the street, stood awaiting the result, and wondering if he could obtain, from the injured man, the receipt which the jailor always gives the slave to take back to his master as evidence of his having been punished.

As the gate opened, and the colored brother made his appearance, looking wildly about for Pompey, the latter called out, "Here I is, sar!"

Maddened by the pain from the excoriation of his bleeding back, and the surprise and astonishment at the quickness with which the whole thing had been accomplished, the man ran across the street, up-braiding in the most furious manner his deceiver,

who also appeared amazed at the epithets bestowed
upon him.

"What have I done to you?" asked Pompey,
with a seriousness that was indeed amusing.

"What hain't you done!" said the man, the tears
streaming down his face. "You've got my back
cut all to pieces," continued the victim.

"What did you let 'em whip you for?" said
Pompey, with a concealed smile.

"You knew that note was to get somebody
whipped, and you put it on me. And here is a
piece of paper that he gave me, and told me to
give it to my master. Just as if I had a master."

"Well, responded Pompey, "I have a half a
dollar, an' I'll give that to you, ef you'll give me
the paper."

Seeing that he could make no better bargain, the
man gave up the receipt, taking in exchange the
silver coin.

"Now," said Pompey, "I'm mighty sorry for ye,
an' ef ye'll go down to de house, I'll pray for ye.
I'm powerful in prayer, dat I is." However the
free man declined Pompey's offer."

"I reckon you'll behave yourself and not spill
the wine over gentlemen again," said Walker, as
Pompey handed him the note from the jailor. "The
next time you commit such a blunder, you'll not get
off so easy," continued the speculator.

Pompey often spoke of the appearance of "my
fren'," as he called the colored brother, and would
enjoy a hearty laugh, saying, "He was a free man,

an' could afford to go to bed, an' lay dar till he got well."

Strangers to the institution of slavery, and its effects upon its victims, would frequently speak with astonishment of the pride that slaves would show in regard to their own value in the market. This was especially so, at auction sales where town or city servants were sold.

"What did your marser pay for you?" would often be asked by one slave of another.

"Eight hundred dollars."

"Eight hundred dollars! Ha, ha! Well, ef I didn't sell for mo' dan eight hundred dollars, I'd neber show my head agin 'mong 'spectable people."

"You got so much to say 'bout me sellin' cheap, now I want to know how much your boss paid fer you?"

"My boss paid fifteen hundred dollars cash, for me; an' it was a rainy day, an' not many out to de auction, or he'd had to pay a heap mo', let me tell you. I'm none of your cheap niggers, I ain't."

"Hy, uncle! Did dey sell you, 'isterday? I see you down dar to de market."

"Yes, dey sole me."

"How much did you fetch?"

"Eighteen hundred dollars."

"Dat was putty smart fer man like you, ain't it?"

"Well, I dunno; it's no mo' dan I is wuf; fer you muss' 'member, I was raised by de Christy's. I'm none of yer common niggers, sellin' fer a picayune. I tink my new boss got me mighty cheap."

"An' so you sole, las' Sataday, fer nine hundred
dollars; so I herd."

"Well, what on it?"

"All I got to say is, ef I was sole, to-morrow, an'
did'nt bring more dan nine hundred dollars, I'd
never look a decent man in de face agin."

These, and other sayings of the kind, were often
heard in any company of colored men, in our
Southern towns.

CHAPTER XII.

THROUGHOUT the Southern States, there are
still to be found remnants of the old time
Africans, who were stolen from their native land
and sold in the Savannah, Mobile, and New Orleans
markets, in defiance of all law. The last-named
city, however, and its vicinity, had a larger portion
of these people than any other section. New Orleans
was their centre, and where their meetings were
not uninteresting.

Congo Square takes its name, as is well known,
from the Congo negroes who used to perform their
dance on its sward every Sunday. They were a
curious people, and brought over with them this
remnant of their African jungles. In Louisiana
there were six different tribes of negroes, named
after the section of the country from which they
came, and their representatives could be seen on the

square, their teeth filed, and their cheeks still bearing tattoo marks. The majority of our city negroes came from the Kraels, a numerous tribe who dwell in stockades. We had here the Minahs, a proud, dignified, warlike race; the Congos, a treacherous, shrewd, relentless people; the Mandringas, a branch of the Congos; the Gangas, named after the river of that name, from which they had been taken; the Hiboas, called by the missionaries the "Owls," a sullen, intractable tribe, and the Foulas, the highest type of the African, with but few representatives here.

These were the people that one would meet on the square many years ago. It was a gala occasion, these Sundays in those years, and not less than two or three thousand people would congregate there to see the dusky dancers. A low fence enclosed the square, and on each street there was a little gate and turnstile. There were no trees then, and the ground was worn bare by the feet of the people. About three o'clock the negroes began to gather, each nation taking their places in different parts of the square. The Minahs would not dance near the Congos, nor the Mandringas near the Gangas. Presently the music would strike up, and the parties would prepare for the sport. Each set had its own orchestra. The instruments were a peculiar kind of banjo, made of a Louisiana gourd, several drums made of a gum stump dug out, with a sheepskin head, and beaten with the fingers, and two jaw-bones of a horse, which when shaken would rattle the loose teeth, keeping time with the drums. About eight negroes, four male and four female, would make a set, and generally they were but scantily clad.

It took some little time before the tapping of the drums would arouse the dull and sluggish dancers, but when the point of excitement came, nothing can faithfully portray the wild and frenzied motions they go through. Backward and forward, this way and that, now together and now apart, every motion intended to convey the most sensual ideas. As the dance progressed, the drums were thrummed faster, the contortions became more grotesque, until sometimes, in frenzy, the women and men would fall fainting to the ground. All this was going on with a dense crowd looking on, and with a hot sun pouring its torrid rays on the infatuated actors of this curious ballet. After one set had become fatigued, they would drop out to be replaced by others, and then stroll off to the groups of some other tribe in a different portion of the square. Then it was that trouble would commence, and a regular set-to with short sticks followed, between the men, and broken heads ended the day's entertainment.

On the sidewalks, around the square, the old negresses, with their spruce-beer and peanuts, cocoanuts and pop-corn, did a thriving trade, and now and then, beneath petticoats, bottles of tafia, a kind of Louisiana rum, peeped out, of which the *gendarmes* were oblivious. When the sun went down, a stream of people poured out of the turn-stiles, and the *gendarmes*, walking through the square, would

order the dispersion of the negroes, and by gun-fire,
at nine o'clock, the place was well-nigh deserted.
These dances were kept up until within the memory
of men still living, and many who believe in them,
and who would gladly revive them, may be found in
every State in the Union.

The early traditions, brought down through the
imported Africans, have done much to keep alive
the belief that the devil is a personal being, with
hoofs, horns, and having powers equal with God.
These ideas give influence to the conjurer, goopher
doctor, and fortune-teller.

While visiting one of the upper parishes, not long
since, I was stopping with a gentleman who was
accustomed to make weekly visits to a neighboring
cemetery, sitting for hours amongst the graves, at
which occurrence the wife felt very sad.

I inquired of her the object of her husband's
strange freak.

"Oh!" said she, "he's influenced out there by
angels."

"Has he gone to the cemetery now?" I asked.

"Yes," was the reply.

"I think I can cure him of it, if you will promise
to keep the whole thing a secret."

"I will," was the reply.

"Let me have a sheet, and unloose your dog, and
I will put the cure in motion," I said. Rolla, the
big Newfoundland dog, was unfastened, the sheet
was well fitted around his neck, tightly sewed, and
the pet told to go hunt his master.

Taking the trail, the dog at once made for the cemetery. Screams of "Help, help! God save me!" coming from the direction of the tombs, aroused the neighborhood. The cries of the man frightened the dog, and he returned home in haste; the sheet, half torn, was removed, and Rolla again fastened in his house.

Very soon Mr. Martin was led in by two friends, who picked him up from the sidewalk, with his face considerably bruised. His story was, that "The devil had chased him out of the cemetery, tripped him up on the sidewalk, and hence the flow of blood from the wound on his face."

The above is a fair index to most of the ghost stories.

CHAPTER XIII.

FORTY years ago, the escapes of slaves from the South, although numerous, were nevertheless difficult, owing to the large rewards offered for their apprehension, and the easy mode of extradition from the Northern States. Little or no difficulty was experienced in capturing and returning a slave from Ohio, Indiana, Illinois, or Pennsylvania, the four States through which the fugitives had to pass in their flight to Canada. The Quaker element in all of the above States showed itself in the furnishing of food to the flying-bondman, concealing him for days, and even weeks, and at last conveying him to a place of safety, or carrying him to the Queen's dominions.

Instinct seemed to tell the negro that a drab coat and a broad-brimmed hat covered a benevolent heart, and we have no record of his ever having been deceived. It is possible that the few Friends scattered over the slave States, and the fact that they were never known to own a slave, gave the blacks a favorable impression of this sect, before the victim of oppression left his sunny birth-place.

A brave and manly slave resolved to escape from Natchez, Miss. This slave, whose name was Jerome, was of pure African origin, was perfectly black, very fine-looking, tall, slim, and erect as any one could possibly be. His features were not bad, lips thin, nose prominent, hands and feet small. His brilliant black eyes lighted up his whole countenance. His hair, which was nearly straight, hung in curls upon his lofty brow. George Combe or Fowler would have selected his head for a model. He was brave and daring, strong in person, fiery in spirit, yet kind and true in his affections, earnest in whatever he undertook.

To reach the free States or Canada, by travelling by night and lying by during the day, from a State so far south as Mississippi, no one would think for a moment of attempting to escape. To remain in the city would be a suicidal step. The deep sound of the escape of steam from a boat, which was at that moment ascending the river, broke upon the

ears of the slave. "If that boat is going up the
river," said he, "why not I conceal myself on board,
and try to escape?" He went at once to the steamboat landing, where the boat was just coming in.
"Bound for Louisville," said the captain, to one
who was making inquiries. As the passengers were
rushing on board, Jerome followed them, and proceeding to where some of the hands were stow-
ing away bales of goods, he took hold and aided
them.

"Jump down into the hold, there, and help the
men," said the mate to the fugitive, supposing that,
like many persons, he was working his way up the
river. Once in the hull, among the boxes, the
slave concealed himself. Weary hours, and at last
days, passed without either water or food with the
hidden slave. More than once did he resolve to let
his case be known; but the knowledge that he would
be sent back to Natchez, kept him from doing so.
At last, with his lips parched and fevered to a crisp,
the poor man crawled out into the freight-room,
and began wandering about. The hatches were on,
and the room dark. There happened to be on board,
a wedding-party; and a box, containing some of the
bridal cake, with several bottles of port wine, was
near Jerome. He found the box, opened it, and
helped himself. In eight days, the boat tied up at
the wharf at the place of her destination. It was
late at night; the boat's crew, with the single exception of the man on watch, were on shore. The
hatches were off, and the fugitive quietly made his

way on deck and jumped on shore. The man saw
the fugitive, but too late to seize him.

Still in a slave State, Jerome was at a loss to know
how he should proceed. He had with him a few
dollars, enough to pay his way to Canada, if he
could find a conveyance. The fugitive procured such
food as he wanted from one of the many eating-
houses, and then, following the direction of the
North Star, he passed out of the city, and took the
road leading to Covington. Keeping near the Ohio
River, Jerome soon found an opportunity to pass
over into the State of Indiana. But liberty was a
mere name in the latter State, and the fugitive learned,
from some colored persons that he met, that it was
not safe to travel by daylight. While making his
way one night, with nothing to cheer him but the
prospect of freedom in the future, he was pounced
upon by three men who were lying in wait for another fugitive, an advertisement of whom they had
received through the mail. In vain did Jerome tell
tell them that he was not a slave. True, they had
not caught the man they expected; but, if they
could make this slave tell from what place he had
escaped, they knew that a good price would be paid
them for the slave's arrest.

Tortured by the slave-catchers, to make him reveal
the name of his owner and the place from whence he
had escaped, Jerome gave them a fictitious name in
Virginia, and said that his master would give a large
reward, and manifested a willingness to return to his
" old boss."

By this misrepresentation, the fugitive hoped to have another chance of getting away.

Allured with the prospect of a large sum of the needful the slave-catchers started back with their victim. Stopping on the second night at an inn, on the banks of the Ohio River, the kidnappers, in lieu of a suitable place in which to confine their prize during the night, chained him to the bed-post of their sleeping chamber.

The white men were late in retiring to rest, after an evening spent in drinking. At dead of night, when all was still, the slave arose from the floor, upon which he had been lying, looked around and saw that Morpheus had possession of his captors. "For once," thought he, "the brandy bottle has done a noble work." With palpitating heart and trembling limbs, he viewed his position. The door was fast, but the warm weather had compelled them to leave the window open. If he could but get the chains off, he might escape through the window to the piazza. The sleepers' clothes hung upon chairs by the bedside. The slave thought of the padlock key, examined the pockets, and found it. The chains were soon off, and the negro stealthily making his way to the window. He stopped, and said to himself, "These men are villains, they are enemies to all who, like me, are trying to be free. Then why not teach them a lesson?" He then dressed himself in the best suit, hung his own worn-out and tattered garments on the same chair, and silently passed through the window to the piazza, and let

himself down by one of the pillars, and started once
more for Canada.

Daylight came upon him before he had selected a
hiding-place for the day, and he was walking at a
rapid rate, in hopes of soon reaching some woodland
or forest. The sun had just begun to show itself,
when Jerome was astonished at seeing behind him,
in the distance, two men upon horseback. Taking
a road to the right he saw before him a farmhouse,
and so near was he to it that he observed two men
in front of him looking at him. It was too late to
turn back. The kidnappers were behind — strange
men before. Those in the rear he knew to be enemies, while he had no idea of what principles were the
farmers. The latter also saw the white men coming,
and called to the fugitive to come that way.

The broad-brimmed hats that the farmers wore
told the slaves that they were Quakers.

Jerome had seen some of these people passing up
and down the river, when employed on a steamer
between Natchez and New Orleans, and had heard
that they disliked slavery. He, therefore, hastened
toward the drab-coated men, who, on his approach,
opened the barn-door, and told him to "run in."

When Jerome entered the barn, the two farmers
closed the door, remaining outside themselves, to
confront the slave-catchers, who now came up and
demanded admission, feeling that they had their prey
secure.

"Thee can't enter my premises," said one of the
Friends, in rather a musical voice.

The negro-catchers urged their claim to the slave, and intimated that, unless they were allowed to secure him, they would force their way in. By this time, several other Quakers had gathered around the barn-door. Unfortunately for the kidnappers, and most fortunately for the fugitive, the Friends had just been holding a quarterly meeting in the neighborhood, and a number of them had not yet returned to their homes.

After some talk, the men in drab promised to admit the hunters, provided they procured an officer and a search-warrant from a justice of the peace. One of the slave-catchers was left to see that the fugitive did not get away, while the other went in pursuit of an officer. In the mean time, the owner of the barn sent for a hammer and nails, and began nailing up the barn-door.

After an hour in search of the man of the law, they returned with an officer and a warrant. The Quaker demanded to see the paper, and, after looking at it for some time, called to his son to go into the house for his glasses. It was a long time before Aunt Ruth found the leather case, and when she did, the glasses wanted wiping before they could be used. After comfortably adjusting them on his nose, he read the warrant over leisurely.

"Come, Mr. Dugdale, we can't wait all day," said the officer.

"Well, will thee read it for me?" returned the Quaker.

The officer complied, and the man in drab said, —

"Yes, thee may go in, now. I am inclined to throw no obstacles in the way of the execution of the law of the land."

On approaching the door, the men found some forty or fifty nails in it, in the way of their progress.

"Lend me your hammer and a chisel, if you please, Mr. Dugdale," said the officer.

"Please read that paper over again, will thee?" asked the Quaker.

The officer once more read the warrant.

"I see nothing there which says I must furnish thee with tools to open my door. If thee wants a hammer, thee must go elsewhere for it; I tell thee plainly, thee can't have mine."

The implements for opening the door are at length obtained, and, after another half hour, the slave-catchers are in the barn. Three hours is a long time for a slave to be in the hands of Quakers. The hay is turned over, and the barn is visited in every part; but still the runaway is not found. Uncle Joseph has a glow upon his countenance; Ephraim shakes his head knowingly; little Elijah is a perfect know-nothing, and if you look toward the house you will see Aunt Ruth's smiling face ready to announce that breakfast is ready.

"The nigger is not in this barn," said the officer.

"I know he is not," quietly remarked the Quaker.

"What were you nailing up your door for, then, as if you were afraid we would enter?" inquired one of the kidnappers.

"I can do what I please with my own door, can't I?" said the Friend.

The secret was out; the fugitive had gone in at the front door, and out at the back; and the reading of the warrant, nailing up of the door, and other preliminaries of the Quaker, was to give the fugitive time and opportunity to escape.

It was now late in the morning, and the slave-catchers were a long way from home, and the horses were jaded by the rapid manner in which they had travelled. The Friends, in high glee, returned to the house for breakfast; the officer and the kidnappers made a thorough examination of the barn and premises, and satisfied that Jerome had gone into the barn, but had not come out, and equally satisfied that he was out of their reach, the owner said, "He's gone down into the earth, and has taken an underground railroad."

And thus was christened that famous highway over which so many of the oppressed sons and daughters of African descent were destined to travel, and an account of which has been published by one of its most faithful agents, Mr. William Still, of Philadelphia.

At a later period, Cato, servant of Dr. Gaines, was sold to Captain Enoch Price, of St. Louis. The Captain took his slave with him on board the steamer *Chester*, just about sailing for New Orleans. At the latter place, the boat obtained a cargo for Cincinnati, Ohio. The master, aware that the slave might give him the slip, while in a free State, determined to leave the chattel at Louisville, Ky., till his downward return. However, Mrs. Price, anxious to have the servant's services on the boat, questioned him with regard to the contemplated visit to Cincinnati.

"I don't want to go to a free State," said Cato; "fer I knowed a servant dat went up dar, once, an' dey kept beggin' him to run away; so I druther not go dar; kase I is satisfied wid my marser, an' don't want to go off, whar I'd have to take keer of mysef."

This was said in such an earnest and off-hand manner, that it removed all of the lady's suspicions in regard to his attempting to escape; and she urged her husband to take him to Ohio.

Cato wanted his freedom, but he well knew that if he expressed a wish to go to a free State, he would never be permitted to do so. In due season, the *Chester* arrived at Cincinnati, where she remained four days, discharging her cargo, and reloading for the return trip. During the time, Cato remained at his post, attending faithfully to his duties; no one dreaming that he had the slightest idea of leaving the boat. However, on the day previous to the *Chester's* leaving Cincinnati, Cato divulged the question to Charley, another slave, whom he wished to accompany him.

Charley heard the proposition with surprise; and although he wanted his freedom, his timid disposition would not allow him to make the trial.

"My master is a pretty good man, and treats me

comparatively well; and should I be caught and taken back, he would no doubt sell me to a cotton or sugar-planter," said Charley to Cato's invitation. "But," continued he, "Captain Price is a mean man; I shall not blame you, Cato, for running away and leaving him. By the by, I am engaged to go to a surprise-party, to-night, and I reckon we'll have a good time. I've got a new pair of pumps to dance in, and I've got Jim, the cook, to bake me a pie, and I'll have some sandwiches, and I'm going with a pretty gal."

"So you won't go away with me, to-night?" said Cato to Charley.

"No," was the reply.

"It is true," remarked Cato, "your marser is a better man, an' treats you a heap better den Captain Price does me, but, den, he may get to gambling, an' get broke, and den he'll have to sell you."

"I know that," replied Charley; "none of us are safe as long as we are slaves."

It was seven o'clock at night, Cato was in the pantry, washing the supper dishes, and contemplating his flight, the beginning of which was soon to take place. Charley had gone up to the steward's hall, to get ready for the surprise, and had been away some time, which caused uneasiness to Cato, and he determined to go up into the cabin, and see that everything was right. Entering the cabin from the Social Hall, Cato, in going down and passing the Captain's room, heard a conversation which attracted his attention, and caused him to halt at his master's room door.

He was not long, although the conversation was in a low tone, in learning that the parties were his master and his fellow-servant Charley.

"And so he is going to run away, to-night, is he?" said the Captain.

"Yes, sir," replied Charley; "he's been trying to get me to go with him, and I thought it my duty to tell you."

"Very well; I'll take him over to Covington, Ky., put him in jail, for the night, and when I get back to New Orleans, I will sell the ungrateful nigger. Where is he now?" asked the Captain.

"Cato is in the pantry, sir, washing up the tea-things," was the reply.

The moving of the chairs in the room, and what he had last heard, satisfied Cato that the talk between his master and the treacherous Charley was at an end, and he at once returned to the pantry undetermined what course to pursue. He had not long been there, ere he heard the well-known squeak of the Captain's boots coming down the stairs. Just then Dick, the cook's boy, came out of the kitchen and threw a pan full of cold meat over-board. This incident seemed to furnish Cato with words, and he at once took advantage of the situation.

"What is dat you throw overboard dar?"

"None your business," replied Dick, as he slammed the door behind him and returned to the kitchen.

"You free niggers will waste everything dar is on dis boat," continued Cato. "It's my duty to watch dees niggers an' see dat dey don't destroy marser's property. Now, let me see, I'll go right off an' tell marser 'bout Charley, I won't keep his secrets any longer." And here Cato threw aside his dish towel and started for the cabin.

Captain Price, who, during Cato's soliloquy, was hid behind a large box of goods, returned in haste to his room, where he was soon joined by his dutiful servant.

In answer to the rap on the door, the Captain said " Come in."

Cato, with downcast look, and in an obsequious manner, entered the room, and said, "Marser, I is come to tell you somethin' dat hangs heavy on my mine, somethin' dat I had ought to tole you afore dis."

"Well," said the master, " what is it, Cato?"

"Now, marser, you hires Charley, don't you?"

"Yes."

"Well, den, ser, ef Charley runs away you'll have to pay fer him, won't you?"

"I think it very probable, as I brought him into a free State, and thereby giving him an opportunity to escape.   Why, is he thinking of running away?"

"Yes, ser," answered Cato, "he's gwine to start to-night, an' he's bin pesterin' me all day to go wid him."

"Do you mean to say that Charley has been trying to persuade you to run away from me?" asked the Captain, rather sharply.

"Yes, ser, dats jess what he's bin a doin' all day.

I axed him whar he's gwine to, an' he sed he's gwine
to Canada, an' he call you some mighty mean names,
an' dat made me mad."

"Why, Charley has just been here telling me that
you were going to run away to-night."

"With apparent surprise, and opening his large
eyes, Cato exclaimed, "Well, well, well, ef dat
nigger don't beat de debble!" And here the negro
raised his hands, and looking upward said, "Afoe
God, marser, I would'nt leave you fer dis worl'.
Now, ser, jess let me tell you how you can find out
who tells de trufe. Charley has got ebry ting ready an'
is a gwine right off. He's got two pies, some sweet-
cake, some sandwiches, bread an' butter, an' he's got
a pair of pumps to dance in when he gets to Canada.
An' ef you want to kotch him in de ack of runnin' away,
you jess wait out on de dock an' you'll kotch him."

This was said in such an earnest manner, and with
such protestations of innocence, that Captain Price
determined to follow Cato's advice and watch for
Charley.

"Go see if you can find where Charley is, and
come back and let me know," said the Captain.

Away went Cato, on his tip-toes, in the direction
of the steward's room, where, by looking through
the key-hole, he saw the treacherous fellow-servant
getting ready for the surprise party that he had
engaged the night previous to attend.

Cato returned almost breathless, and in a whisper
said, "I foun' him ser, he's gittin' ready to start.
He's got a bundle of provisions tied up all ready, ser;

you'll be shur to kotch him as he's gwine away, ef you go on de dock."

Throwing his camlet cloak over his shoulders, the Captain passed out upon the wharf, took a position behind a pile of wood, and awaited the coming of the negro; nor did he remain long in suspense.

With lighted cigar, dressed in his best apparel, and his eatables tied up in a towel, Charley was soon seen hastily leaving the boat.

Stepping out from his hiding-place, the Captain seized the negro by the collar and led him back to the steamer, exclaiming, "Where are you going, what's that you've got in that bundle?"

"Only some washin' I is takin' out to get done," replied the surprised and frightened negro.

As they reached the lighted deck, "Open that bundle," said the Captain.

Charley began to obey the command, and at the the same time to give an explanation.

"Shut your mouth, you scoundrel," vociferously shouted the Captain.

As the man slowly undid the parcel, and the contents began to be seen, "There," said .the Captain, "there's the pies, cake, sandwiches, bread and butter that Cato told me you had put up to eat while running away. Yes, there's the pumps, too, that you got to dance in when you reached Canada."

Here the frightened Charley attempted again to explain, "I was jess gwine to—"

"Shut your mouth, you villain; you were going to escape to Canada."

"No, Marser Price, afoe God I was only—"

"Shut your mouth, you black rascal; you told me you were taking some clothes to be washed, you lying scamp."

During this scene, Cato was inside the pantry, with the door ajar, looking out upon his master and Charley with unfeigned satisfaction.

Still holding the negro by the collar, and leading him to the opposite side of the boat, the Captain called to Mr. Roberts, the second mate, to bring up the small boat to take him and the "runaway" over the river.

A few moments more, and the Captain, with Charley seated by his side, was being rowed to Covington, where the negro was safely locked up for the night.

"A little longer," said the Captain to the second officer, as he returned to the boat, "a little longer and I'd a lost fifteen hundred dollars by that boy's running away."

"Indeed," responded the officer.

"Yes," continued the Commander, "my servant Cato told me, just in time to catch the rascal in the very act of running off."

One of the sailors who was rowing, and who had been attentively listening to the Captain, said, "I overheard Cato to-day, trying to persuade Charley to go somewhere with him to-night, and the latter said he was going to a 'surprise party.' "

"The devil you did," exclaimed the Captain. "Hasten up there," continued he, "for these niggers are a slippery set."

"As the yawl came alongside of the steamer, Captain Price leaped on deck and went directly in search of Cato, who could nowhere be found. And even Charley's bundle, which he left where he had been opening it, was gone. All search for the tricky man was in vain.

On the following morning, Charley was brought back to the boat, saying, as they were crossing the river, "I tole de boss dat Cato was gwine to run away, but he did'nt bleve me. Now he sees Cato's gone."

After the Captain had learned all that he could from Charley, the latter's account of his imprisonment in the lock-up caused great merriment amongst the boat's crew.

"But I tell you dar was de biggest rats in dat jail, eber I seed in my life. Dey run aroun' dar an' make so much fuss dat I was 'fraid to set down or lay down. I had to stan' up all night."

The *Chester* was detained until in the latter part of the day, during which time every effort was made to hunt up Cato, but without success.

When upbraided by the black servants on the boat for his treachery to Cato, Charley's only plea was, "I 'speck it was de debble dat made me do it."

Dressing himself in his warmest and best clothes, and getting some provisions that he had prepared during the day, and also taking with him Charley's pies, cakes, sandwiches, and pumps, Cato left the boat and made good his escape before his master returned from Covington.

It was during the cold winter of 1834, that the fugitive travelled by night and laid by in the woods in the day. After a week's journey, his food gave out, and then came the severest of his trials, cold coupled with hunger.

Often Cato would resolve to go to some of the farm-houses and apply for food and shelter, but the fear of being captured and again returned prevented him from following his inclinations. One night a pelting rain that froze as fast as it fell, drove the fugitive into a barn, where, creeping under the hay, he remained, sleeping sweetly while his garments were drying upon his person.

Sounds of the voices of the farmer and his men feeding the cattle and doing the chores, awakened the man from his slumbers, who, seeing that it was daylight, feared he would be arrested. However, the day passed, and the fugitive coming out at night-fall, started once more on his weary journey, taking for his guide the North Star, and after travelling the entire night, he again lay by, but this time in the forest.

Three days of fasting had now forced hunger upon Cato, so that he once more determined to seek food. Waiting till night, he came upon the highway, and soon approached a farm-house, of the olden style, built of logs. The sweet savor of the supper attracted the hungry man's attention as he neared the dwelling. For once there was no dog to herald his coming, and he had an opportunity of viewing the interior of the house, through the apertures that a log cabin generally presents.

As the fugitive stood with one eye gazing through the *crack*, looking at the table, already set, and snuffing in the delicious odor from a boiling pot, he heard the mother say,—"Take off the chicken, Sally Ann, I guess the dumplings are done. Your father will be home in half an hour; if he should catch that nigger and bring him along, we'll feed him on the cold meat and potatoes."

With palpitating heart, Cato listened to the last sentences that fell from the woman's lips. Who could the "nigger" be, thought he.

Finding only the woman and her daughter in the house, the black man had been debating in his own mind whether or not to go in and demand a part of the contents of the kettle. However, the talk about "catching a nigger," settled the question at once with him.

Seizing a sheet that hung upon the clothes-line, Cato covered himself with it; leaving open only enough to enable him to see, he rushed in, crying at the top of his voice,—"Come to judgment! Come to judgment."

Both women sprang from their seats, and, screaming, passed out of the room, upsetting the table as they went. Cato seized the pot of chicken with one hand, and a loaf of bread, that had fallen from the table, with the other; hastily leaving the house and taking to the road, he continued on his journey.

The fugitive, however, had gone but a short distance when he heard the tramp of horses and the voices of men; and, fearing to meet them, he took to the woods till they had passed by.

As he hid behind a large tree by the roadside, Cato heard distinctly:

"And what is your master's name?"

"Peter Johnson, ser," was the reply.

"How much do you think he will give to have you brought back?"

"Dunno, ser," responded a voice which Cato recognized by the language to be a negro.

It was evident that a fugitive slave had been captured, and was about to be returned for the reward. And it was equally evident to Cato that the slave had been caught by the owner of the pot of stewed chicken that he then held in his hand, and he felt a thrill of gladness as he returned to the road and pursued his journey.

CHAPTER XIV.

IN the year 1850, there were fifty thousand free colored people in the slave States, the greater number residing in Louisiana, Maryland, Virginia, Tennessee, and South Carolina. In all the States these people were allowed but few privileges not given to the slaves; and in many their condition was thought to be even worse than that of the bondmen. Laws, the most odious, commonly known as the "Black Code," were enacted and enforced in every

State. These provided for the punishment of the free colored people — punishment which was not mentioned in the common law for white persons; for binding out minors, a species of slavery, and naming thirty-two offences more for blacks than had been enacted for the whites, and eight of which made it capital punishment for the offences committed.

Public opinion, which is often stronger than law, was severe in the extreme. In many of the Southern cities, including Charleston, S. C., a colored lady, free, and owning the fine house in which she lived, was not allowed to wear a veil in the public streets.

In passing through the thoroughfares, blacks of both sexes were compelled to take the outside, on pain of being kicked into the street, or sent to the lock-up and whipped.

As late as 1858, a movement was made in several of the Southern States to put an exorbitant tax upon them, and in lieu of which they were to be sold into life-long slavery. Maryland led off with a bill being introduced into the Legislature by Mr. Hover, of Frederick County, for levying a tax of two dollars per annum on all colored male inhabitants of the State over twenty-one years of age, and under fifty-five, and of one dollar on every female over eighteen and under forty-five, to be collected by the collectors of the State taxes, and *devoted to the use of the Colonization Society*. In case of the refusal to pay of a property-holder or housekeeper, his or her goods were to be seized and sold; if not a property-holder, the body of the non-paying person was to be seized, and hired out to the lowest bidder who would agree to pay the tax; and in case of not being able to hire said delinquents out, they were to be sold to any person who would pay the amount of tax and costs for the lowest period of service!

Tennessee followed in the same strain. The annexed protest of one of her noblest sons,—Judge Catron, appeared at the time. He said:

"My objection to the bill is, *that it proposes to commit an outrage, to perpetrate an oppression and cruelty.* This is the plain truth, and it is idle to mince words to soften the fact. Let us look the proposition boldly in the face. This depressed and helpless portion of our population is designed to be driven out, or to be enslaved for life, and their property forfeited, as no slave can hold property. The mothers are to be sold, or driven away from their children, many of them infants. The children are to be bound out until they are twenty-one years of age, and then to leave the State or be sold; which means that they are to be made slaves for life, in fact. Now, of these women and children, there is hardly one in ten that is of unmixed negro blood. Some are half-white; many have half-white mothers and white fathers, making a cast of 87 1-2–100ths of white blood; many have a third cross, in whom the negro blood is almost extinct; such is the unfortunate truth. This description of people, who were born free, and lived as free persons, are to be introduced as slaves into our families, or into our negro

quarters, there to be under an overseer, or they are
to be sold to the negro-trader and sent South, there
to be whipped by overseers — *and to preach rebellion*
in the negro quarters — as they will *preach* rebellion
everywhere that they may be driven to by this unjust law, whether it be amongst us here in Tennessee
or south of us on the cotton and sugar plantations,
or in the abolition meetings in the free States. Nor
will the women be the least effective in preaching a
crusade, when begging money in the North, to relieve
their children, left behind in this State, in bondage.

"We are told that this 'free-negro bill" is a politic,
popular measure. Where is it popular? *In what
nook or corner of the State are principles of humanity so deplorably deficient that a majority of the
whole inhabitants would commit an outrage not committed in a Christian country of which history gives
any account?* In what country is it, this side of
Africa, that the majority have enslaved the minority,
sold the weak to the strong, and applied the pro-
ceeds of the sale to educate the children of the
stronger side, as this bill proposes? It is an open
assertion that 'might makes right.' It is re-opening the
African slave trade. In that trade the strong capture the weak, and sell them ; and so it will be here,
if this policy is carried out."

In some of the States the law was enacted and
the people driven out or sold. Those who were able
to pay their way out, came away ; those who could
not raise the means, were doomed to languish in
bondage till released by the Rebellion.

About the same time, in Georgia, Florida, and South Carolina, strong efforts were being made to re-open the African slave trade. At the Democratic State Convention, held in the city of Charleston, S. C., May 1, 1860, Mr. Gaulden made the following speech : —

"MR. PRESIDENT, AND FELLOW DEMOCRATS : — As I stated to you a few moments ago, I have been confined to my room by severe indisposition, but learning of the commotion and the intense excitement which were existing upon the questions before this body, I felt it to be my duty, feeble as I was, to drag myself out to the meeting of my delegation, and when there I was surprised to find a large majority of that delegation voting to secede at once from this body. I disagree with those gentlemen. I regret to disagree with my brethren from the South upon any of the great questions which interest our common country. I am a Southern States' Rights man ; I am an African slave-trader. I believe I am one of those Southern men who believe that slavery is right, morally, religiously, socially, and politically. (Applause.) I believe that the institution of slavery has done more for this country, more for civilization, than all other interests put together. I believe if it were in the power of this country to strike down the institution of slavery, it would put civilization back two hundred years. I tell you, fellow Democrats, that the African slave-trader is the true Union man. (Cheers and laughter.) I tell you that the slave-trading of Virginia is more im-

moral, more un-Christian in every possible point of
view, than that African slave-trade which goes to
Africa and brings a heathen and worthless man here,
makes him a useful man, Christianizes him, and
sends him and his posterity down the stream of
time to join in the blessings of civilization.   (Cheers
and laughter.)   Now, fellow-democrats, so far as
any public expression of opinion of the State of
Virginia—the great slave-trading State of Virginia
—has been given, they are all opposed to the
African slave-trade."

Dr. REED, of Indiana.—I am from Indiana, and
I am in favor of it.

MR. GAULDEN.—Now, gentlemen, we are told,
upon high authority, that there is a certain class of
men who strain at a gnat and swallow a camel.
Now, Virginia, which authorizes the buying of
Christian men, separating them from their wives
and children, from all the relations and associations
amid whom they have lived for years, rolls up·her
eyes in holy horror when I would go to Africa, buy
a savage, and introduce him to the blessings of
civilization and Christianity.   (Cheers and laughter.)

MR. RYNDERS, of New York.—You can get one
or two recruits from New York to join with you.

THE PRESIDENT.—The time of the gentleman has
expired.   (Cries of "Go on! go on!")

The President stated that if it was the unanimous
wish of the Convention, the gentleman could proceed.

MR. GAULDEN.—Now, fellow Democrats, the

slave-trade in Virginia forms a mighty and powerful reason for its opposition to the African slave-trade, and in this remark I do not intend any disrespect to my friends from Virginia. Virginia, the Mother of States and of statesmen, the Mother of Presidents, I apprehend, may err as well as other mortals. I am afraid that her error in this regard lies in the promptings of the almighty dollar. It has been my fortune to go into that noble old State to buy a few darkies, and I have had to pay from one thousand to two thousand dollars a head, when I could go to Africa and buy better negroes for fifty dollars a-piece. (Great laughter.) Now, unquestionably, it is to the interests of Virginia to break down the African slave-trade when she can sell her negroes at two thousand dollars. She knows that the African slave-trade would break up her monopoly, and hence her objection to it. If any of you Northern Democrats —for I have more faith in you than I have in the Carpet Knight Democracy of the South—will go home with me to my plantation in Georgia, but a little way from here, I will show you some darkies that I bought in Maryland, some that I bought in Virginia, some in Delaware, some in Florida, some in North Carolina, and I will also show you the pure African, the noblest Roman of them all. (Great laughter.) Now, fellow Democrats, my feeble health and failing voice admonish me to bring the few remarks I have to make to a close. (Cries of "Go on! go on!") I am only sorry that I am not in a better condition than I am to vindicate before you to-day the words of truth, of honesty, and of right, and to show you the gross inconsistencies of the South in this regard. I came from the First Congressional District of the State of Georgia. I represent the African slave-trade interests of that section. (Applause.) I am proud of the position I occupy in that respect. I believe that the African slave-trader is a true missionary, and a true Christian. (Applause.)

Such was the feeling in a large part of the South, with regard to the enslavement of the negro.

CHAPTER XV.

THE success of the slave-holders in controlling the affairs of the National Government for a long series of years, furnishing a large majority of the Presidents, Speakers of the House of Representatives, Foreign Ministers, and moulding the entire policy of the nation in favor of slave-holding, and the admitted fact that none could secure an office in the national Government who were known to be opposed to the *peculiar* institution, made the Southerners feel themselves superior to the people of the free States. This feeling was often manifested by an outburst of intemperate language, which frequently showed itself in the pulpit, on the rostrum, and in the drawing-room. On all such occasions the placing of the institution of slavery above liberty, seemed to be the aim of its advocates.

"The principle of slavery is in itself right, and *does not depend on difference of complexion*," — said the Richmond (Va.) *Enquirer*.

A distinguished Southern statesman exclaimed, —

"Make the laboring man the slave of *one* man, instead of the slave of society, and he would be far better off." "Slavery, *black or white*, is right and necessary." "*Nature has made the weak in mind or body for slaves.*"

Another said : —

"*Free* society ! We sicken of the name. What is it but a conglomeration of *greasy mechanics, filthy operators, small-fisted farmers*, and moonstruck theorists? All the Northern States, and especially the New England States, are *devoid of society fitted for well-bred gentlemen*. The prevailing class one meets with is that of mechanics struggling to be genteel, and small farmers, who do their own drudgery; and yet who are hardly fit for association with a gentleman's body servant [slave]. This is your free society."

The insults offered to John P. Hale and Charles Sumner in the United States Senate, and to Joshua R. Giddings and Owen Lovejoy in the House of Representatives, were such as no legislative body in the world would have allowed, except one controlled by slave-drivers. I give the following, which may be taken as a fair specimen of the *bulldozing* of those days.

In the National House of Representatives Hon. O. Lovejoy, member from Illinois, was speaking against the further extension of slavery in the territories, when he was interrupted by Mr. Barksdale, of Mississippi —

"Order that black-hearted scoundrel and nigger-stealing thief to take his seat."

By Mr. Boyce, of South Carolina, addressing Mr. Lovejoy —

"Then behave yourself."

By Mr. Gartrell, of Georgia, (in his seat) —

"The man is crazy."

By Mr. Barksdale, of Mississippi, again —

"No, sir; you stand there to-day, an infamous, perjured villain."

By Mr. Ashmore, of South Carolina —

"Yes; he is a perjured villain, and he perjures himself every hour he occupies a seat on this floor."

By Mr. Singleton, of Mississippi —

"And a negro thief into the bargain."

By Mr. Barksdale, of Mississippi, again —

"I hope my colleague will hold no parley with that perjured negro thief."

By Mr. Singleton, of Mississippi, again —

"No sir; any gentleman shall have time, but not such a mean, despicable wretch as that."

By Mr. Martin, of Virginia —

"And if you come among us, we will do with you as we did with John Brown — hang you as high as Haman. I say that as a Virginian."

Hon. Robert Toombs, of Georgia, made a violent

speech in the Senate, January, 1860, in which he said : —

"*Never permit this Federal Government to pass into the traitorous hands of the Black Republican party.*" It has already declared war against you and your institutions. It every day commits acts of war against you; it has already compelled you to arm for your defence. Listen to 'no vain babblings,' to no treacherous jargon about 'overt acts;' they have already been committed. Defend yourselves; the enemy is at your door; wait not to meet him at the hearthstone, — meet him at the door-sill, and drive him from the temple of liberty, or pull down its pillars and involve him in a common ruin."

Such and similar sentiments expressed at the South, and even by Southerners when sojourning in the free States, did much to widen the breach, and to bring on the conflict of arms that soon followed.

CHAPTER XVI.

THE night was dark, the rain descended in torrents from the black and overhanging clouds, and the thunder, accompanied with vivid flashes of lightning, resounded fearfully, as I entered a negro cabin in South Carolina. The room was filled with blacks, a group of whom surrounded a rough board table, and at it sat an old man holding in his hand a watch, at which all were intently gazing. A stout negro boy held a torch which lighted up the cabin, and near him stood a Yankee soldier, in the Union blue, reading the President's Proclamation of Freedom.

As it neared the hour of twelve, a dead silence prevailed, and the holder of the time-piece said, — "By de time I counts ten, it will be midnight an' de lan' will be free. One, two, three, four, five, six, seven, eight, nine, — " just then a loud strain of music came from the banjo, hanging upon the wall, and at its sound the whole company, as if by previous arrangement, threw themselves upon their knees, and the old man exclaimed, — "O, God, de watch was a minit' too slow, but dy promises an' dy mercy is allers in time; dou did promise dat one of dy angels should come an' give us de sign, an' shore 'nuff de sign did come. We's grateful, O, we's grateful, O, Lord, send dy angel once moe to give dat sweet sound."

At this point another strain from the banjo was heard, and a sharp flash of lightning was followed by a clap of thunder, such as is only heard in the tropics. The negroes simultaneously rose to their feet and began singing; finishing only one verse, they all fell on their knees, and Uncle Ben, the old white-haired man, again led in prayer, and such a prayer as but few outside of this injured race could have given. Rising to their feet, the leader commenced singing : —

" Oh ! breth-er-en, my way, my way's cloudy, my way,
        Go send dem angels down.
Oh ! breth-er-en, my way, my way's cloudy, my way,
        Go send dem angels down.
There's fire in de east an' fire in de west,
        Send dem angels down.
An' fire among de Methodist,
        O, send dem angels down.
Ole Sa-tan's mad, an' I am glad,
        Send dem angels down.
He missed the soul he thought he had,
        O, send dem angels down.
I'll tell you now as I tole afore,
        Send dem angels down.
To de promised lan' I'm bound to go,
        O, send dem angels down.
Dis is de year of Jubilee,
        Send dem angels down.
De Lord has come to set us free,
        O, send dem angels down."

One more short prayer from Uncle Ben, and they
arose, clasped each other around the neck, kissed,
and commenced shouting, " Glory to God, we's free."

Another sweet strain from the musical instrument
was followed by breathless silence, and then Uncle
Ben said, "De angels of de Lord is wid us still, an'
dey is watching ober us, fer ole Sandy tole us moe
dan a mont ago dat dey would."

I was satisfied when the first musical strain came,
that it was merely a vibration of the strings, caused
by the rushing wind through the aperture between
the logs behind the banjo.   Fearing that the blacks

would ascribe the music to some mysterious Providence, I plainly told them of the cause.

"Oh, no ser," said Uncle Ben, quickly, his eyes brightening as he spoke, "dat come fum de angels. We been specken it all de time. We know the angels struck the strings of de banjo."

The news of the music from the instrument without the touch of human hands soon spread through the entire neighborhood, and in a short time the cabin was jammed with visitors, who at once turned their attention to the banjo upon the wall.

All sorts of stories were soon introduced to prove that angelic visits were common, especially to those who were fortunate enough to carry "de witness."

"De speret of de Lord come to me lass night in my sleep an' tole me dat I were gwine to be free, an' sed dat de Lord would sen' one of His angels down to give me de warnin'. An' when de banjo sounded, I knowed dat my bressed Marster were a' keepin' His word," said Uncle Ben.

An elderly woman amongst the visitors, drew a long breath, and declared that she had been lifted out of her bed three times on the previous night; "I knowed," she continued, "dat de angelic hoss was hoverin' round about us."

"I dropped a fork to-day," said another, "an' it stuck up in de floo', right afore my face, an' dat is allers good luck fer me."

"De mule kicked at me three times dis mornin' an' he never did dat afore in his life," said another, "an' I knowed good luck would come fum dat."

"A rabbit run across my path twice as I come fum de branch lass Saturday, an' I felt shor' dat somethin' mighty was gwine to happen," remarked Uncle Ben's wife.

"I had a sign that showed me plainly that all of you would be free," said the Yankee soldier, who had been silent since reading the proclamation. All eyes were instantly turned to the white man from the North, and half a dozen voices cried out simultaneously, "O, Mr. Solger, what was it? what was it? what was it?"

"Well," said the man in blue, "I saw something on a large white sheet — "

"Was it a goos?"-cried Uncle Ben, before the sentence was finished by the soldier. Uncle Ben's question about a ghost, started quite a number to their feet, and many trembled as they looked each other in the face, and upon the soldier, who appeared to feel the importance of his position.

Ned, the boy who was holding the torch, began to tell a ghost story, but he was at once stopped by Uncle Ben, who said, "Shet your mouf, don't you see de gentmun ain't told us what he see in de 'white sheet?'"

"Well," commenced the soldier, again, "I saw on a large sheet of paper, a printed Proclamation from President Lincoln, like the one I've just read, and that satisfied me that you'd all be free to-day."

Every one was disappointed at this, for all were prepared for a ghost story, from the first remark about the "white sheet" of paper. Uncle Ben smiled, looked a little wise, and said, "I speck dat's a Yankee trick you's given us, Mr. Solger."

The laugh of the man in blue was only stopped by Uncle Ben's striking up the following hymn, in which the whole company joined : —

" A storm am brewin' in de Souf,
    A storm am brewin' now.
Oh! hearken den, and shut your mouf,
    And I will tell you how :
And I will tell you how, ole boy,
    De storm of fire will pour,
And make de black folks sing for joy,
    As dey neber sing afore.

" So shut your mouf as close as deafh,
    And all you niggas hole your breafh,
        And do de white folks brown!

" De black folks at de Norf am ris,
    And dey am comin' down —
And comin' down, I know dey is,
    To do de white folks brown!
Dey'll turn ole Massa out to grass,
    And set de niggas free,
And when dat day am come to pass
    We'll all be dar to see!

" So shut your mouf as close as deafh,
    And all you niggas hole your breafh,
        And I will tell you how.

" Den all de week will be as gay
    As am de Chris'mas time ;

We'll dance all night and all de day,
      And make de banjo chime,
And make de banjo chime, I tink,
      And pass de time away,
Wid 'nuf to eat and 'nuf to drink,
      And not a bit to pay!

" So shut your mouf as close as deaf h,
      And all you niggas hole your breaf h,
      And make de banjo chime."

However, there was in this company, a man some
forty years old, who, like a large number of the
slaves, had been separated in early life from his
relatives, and was now following in the wake of the
Union army, hoping to meet some of those dear
ones.

This was Mark Myers. At the age of twenty he
fled from Winchester, Va., and although pursued by
bloodhounds, succeeded in making good his escape.
The pursuers returned and reported that Mark had
been killed. This story was believed by all.

Now the war had opened the way, Mark had
come from Michigan, as a servant for one of the
officers; Mark followed the army to Harper's Ferry,
and then went up to Winchester. Twenty years
had caused a vast change, and although born and
brought up there, he found but few that could tell
him anything about the old inhabitants.

"Go to an ole cabin at de edge of de town, an'
darh you'll find ole Unkel Bob Smart, an' he know
ebbrybody, man an boy, dat's lived here for forty

years," said an old woman of whom he inquired. With haste Mark proceeded to the " ole cabin," and there he found "Unkel Bob."

"Yer say yer name is Mark Myers, an' yer mamma's name is Nancy," responded the old man to the inquiries put to him by Mark.

"Yes," was the reply.

"Well, sonney," continued Uncle Bob, "de Myers niggers was all sold to de traders 'bout de beginnin' ov de war, septin some ov de ole ones dat dey couldn't sell, an' I specks yer mamma is one ov dem dat de traders didn't want. Now, sonney, yer go over to de Redman place, an' it 'pers to me dat de oman yer's lookin' fer is over darh."

Thanking Uncle Bob, Mark started for the farm designated by the old man. Arriving there, he was told that "Aunt Nancy lived over yarnder on de wess road." Proceeding to the low log hut, he entered, and found the woman.

"Is this Aunt Nancy Myers?"

"Yes, sar, dis is me."

"Had you a son named Mark?"

"Yes, dat I did, an' a good boy he were, poor feller." And here the old woman wiped the tears away with the corner of her apron.

"I have come to bring you some good news about him."

"Good news 'bout who?" eagerly asked the woman.

"Good news about your son Mark."

"Oh! no; you can't bring me no good news 'bout my son, septin you bring it from hebben, fer I feel

sartin dat he is darh, fer he suffered nuff when de
dogs killed him, to go to hebben."

Mark had already recognized his mother, and
being unable to longer conceal the fact, he seized
her by the hand and said :

"Mother, don't you know me? I am your long-
lost son Mark."

Amazed at the sudden news, the woman trembled
like a leaf, the tears flowed freely, and she said :

"My son, Mark, had a deep gash across the
bottom of his left foot, dat he will take wid him
to his grave. Ef you is my son, show me de
mark."

As quick almost as thought, Mark pulled off his
boot, threw himself on the floor and held up the
foot. The old woman wiped her glasses, put them
on, saw the mark of the deep gash ; then she fainted,
and fell at her son's side.

Neighbors flocked in from the surrounding huts,
and soon the cabin was filled with an eager crowd,
who stood in breathless silence to catch every word
that should be spoken. As the old woman revived,
and opened her eyes, she tremblingly said :

"My son, it is you."

"Yes, mother," responded the son, "it is me.
When I ran away, old master put the dogs upon my
track, but I jumped into the creek, waded down for
some distance, and by that means the dogs lost the
scent, and I escaped from them."

"Well," said the old woman, "in my prayers I
axed God to permit me to meet you in hebben, an'

He promised me I should ; but He's bin better den His promise."

"Now, mother, I have a home for you at the North, and I have come to take you to it."

The few goods worth bringing away from the slave hut were soon packed up, and ere the darkness had covered the land, mother and son were on their way to the North.

CHAPTER XVII.

DURING the Rebellion and at its close, there was one question that appeared to overshadow all others ; this was Negro Equality. While the armies were on the field of battle, this was the great bugbear among many who warmly espoused the cause of the Government, and who approved all its measures, with this single exception. They sincerely wished the rebels to be despoiled of their property. They wished every means to be used to secure our success on the field, including Emancipation. But they would grow pale at the words Negro Equality ; just as if the liberating of a race, and securing to them personal, political, social and religious rights, made it incumbent upon us to take these people into our houses, and give them seats in our social circle, beyond what we would accord to other total strangers. No advocate of Negro Equality ever demanded for the race that they should be made pets. Protect them in their natural, lawful, and acquired rights, is all they ask.

Social equality is a condition of society that must make itself. There are colored families residing in every Southern State, whose education and social position is far above a large portion of their neighboring whites. To compel them to associate with these whites would be a grievous wrong. Then, away with this talk, which is founded in hatred to an injured people. Give the colored race in the South equal protection before the law, and then we say to them—

> " Now, to gain the social prize,
> Paddle your own canoe."

But this hue and cry about Negro Equality generally emanates from a shoddy aristocracy, or an uneducated class, more afraid of the negro's ability and industry than of his color rubbing off against them,—men whose claims to equality are so frail that they must be fenced about, and protected by every possible guard ; while the true nobleman fears not that his reputation will be compromised by any association he may choose to form. So it is with many of those men who fear negro competition. Conscious of their own inferiority to the mass of mankind, and recognizing the fact that they exist and thrive only by the aid of adventitious advantages, they look with jealousy on any new rivals and competitors, and use every means, fair and unfair, to keep them out of the market.

The same sort of opposition has been made to the introduction of female labor into any of the various branches of manufacture. Consequently, women have always been discriminated against. They have been restricted to a small range of employments; their wages have been kept down; and many who would be perfectly competent to perform the duties of clerks or accountants, or to earn good wages in some branch of manufacture, have been driven by their necessities either to suicide or prostitution.

But the nation, knowing the Southerners as they did, aware of the deep hatred to Northern whites, and still deeper hatred to their ex-slaves, who aided in blotting out the institution of slavery, it was the duty of the nation, having once clothed the colored man with the rights of· citizenship and promised him in the Constitution full protection for those rights, to keep this promise most sacredly. The question, while it is invested with equities of the most sacred character, is not without its difficulties and embarrassments. Under the policy adopted by the Democrats in the late insurrectionary States, the colored citizen has been subjected to a reign of terror which has driven him from the enjoyment of his rights and leaves him as much a nonenity in politics, unless he obeys their behests, as he was when he was in slavery. Under this condition of things to-day, while he if properly protected in his rights would hold political supremacy in Mississippi, Georgia, South Carolina, Louisiana, Alabama, and

Florida, he has little or no voice in either State or National Government.

Through fear, intimidation, assassination, and all the horrors that barbarism can invent, every right of the negro in the Southern States is to-day at an end. Complete submission to the whites is the only way for the colored man to live in peace.

Some time since there was considerable talk about a " War of Races," but the war was all on the side

KU-KLUX EMBLEMS.

of the whites. The freedman has succumbed to brute force, and hence the war of races is suspended ; but let him attempt to assert his rights of citizenship, as the white man does at the North, according to the dictates of his own conscience and sense of duty, and the bloody hands of the Ku-Klux and White Leaguer will appear in all their horrors once more — the " dream that has passed " would become a sad reality again.

CHAPTER XVIII.

IMMEDIATELY after the Rebellion ceased, the freedmen throughout the South, desiring no doubt to be fully satisfied that they were actually free and their own masters, and could go where they pleased, left their homes in the country and took up their abode in the cities and towns. This, as a matter of course, threw them out of business, and large numbers could be seen idly lolling about the steps of the court house, town hall, or other county buildings, or listlessly wandering through the streets. That they were able to do this seemed to them positive evidence that they were really free. It was not long, however, before they began to discover that they could not live without work, and that the only labor that they understood was in the country on the plantations. Consequently they returned to the farms, and in many instances to their former masters. Yet the old love for visiting the cities and towns remained, and they became habituated to leaving their work on Saturdays, and going to the place nearest to them. This caused Saturday to be called "nigger day," in most of the Southern States.

On these occasions they sell their cotton or other produce, do their trading, generally having two jugs, one for the molasses, the other for the whiskey, as indispensible to the visit. The store-keepers get ready on Saturday morning, putting their brightest and most gaudy-colored goods in the windows or on the front of their counters. Jew shops put their hawkers at their doors, and the drinking saloons, billiard saloons, and other places of entertainment, kept for their especial accommodation, either by men of their own race or by whites, are all got ready for an extra run.

Being on a visit to the State of Alabama, for a while, I had a fair opportunity of seeing the colored people in that section under various circumstances. It was in the autumn and I was at Huntsville. The principal business houses of the city are situated upon a square which surrounds the court house, and at an early hour in the morning this is filled with colored people of all classes and shades. On Saturdays there are often fully two thousand of them in the streets at one time. At noon the throng was greatest, and up to that time fresh wagon-loads of men, women, and children, were continually arriving. They came not only in wagons, but on horses, and mules, and on foot. Their dress and general appearance were very dissimilar. Some were dressed in a queer looking garment made of pieces of old army blankets, a few were apparelled in faded military overcoats, which were liberally supplied with patches of other material. The women, unlike their husbands and other male relations, were dressed in finery of every conceivable fashion. All of them were decked out with many-colored ribbons. They wore pinchbeck jewelry in large quantities. A few of the young girls displayed some little taste in the arrangement of their dress; and some of them wore expensive clothes. These, however, were "city niggers," and found but little favor in the eyes of the country girls. As the farmers arrived they hitched their tumble-down wagons and bony mules

near the court house, and then proceeded to dispose
of the cotton and other products which they had
brought to town.

While the men are selling their effects, the women
go about from store to store, looking at the many
gaudy articles of wearing apparel which cunning
shop-keepers have spread out to tempt their fancy.
As soon as "the crop" is disposed of, and a negro
farmer has money in his pocket, his first act is to pay
the merchant from whom he obtained his supplies
during the year. They are improvident and ignorant sometimes, but it must be said, to their credit,
that as a class they always pay their debts, the
moment they are in a position to do so. The country would not be so destitute if a larger number of
white men followed their example in this respect.
When they have settled up all their accounts, and
arranged for future bills, they go and hunt up their
wives, who are generally on the look-out. They
then proceed to a dining saloon, call for an expensive meal, always finishing with pies, puddings, or
preserves, and often with all three. When they
have satisfied their appetites, they go first to the
dry-goods stores. Here, as in other shops, they are
met by obsequious white men, who conduct them at
once to a back or side room, with which most of the
stores are supplied. At first I could not fathom the
mystery of this ceremony. After diligent inquiry,
however, I discovered that, since the war, unprinci-
pled store-keepers, some of them northern men,
have established the custom of giving the country

negroes, who come to buy, as much whiskey as they wish to drink. This is done in the back rooms I have mentioned, and when the unfortunate black men and women are deprived of half their wits by the vile stuff which is served out to them, they are induced to purchase all sorts of useless and expensive goods.

In their soberest moments average colored women have a passion for bright, colored dresses which amounts almost to madness, and, on such occasions as I have mentioned, they never stop buying until their money is exhausted. Their husbands have little or no control over them, and are obliged, whether they will or not, to see most of their hard earnings squandered upon an unserviceable jacket, or flimsy bonnet, or many-colored shawl. I saw one black woman spend upward of thirty dollars on millinery goods. As she received her bundle from the cringing clerk she said, with a laugh :

"I 'clare to the Lord I'se done gone busted my old man, sure."

"Never mind," said the clerk, "he can work for more."

"To be sure," answered the woman, and then flounced out of the store.

The men are but little better than the women in their extravagance. I saw a man on the square who had bargained for a mule, which he very much needed, and which he had been intending to purchase as soon as he sold his cotton. He agreed to pay fifty-seven dollars for the animal, and felt in his pocket for the money, but could find only sixteen dollars. Satisfying himself that he had no more, he said:

"Well, well, ef dis ain't de most stravagant nigger I ever see; I sole two bales of cotton dis bressed day, an' got one hundred and twenty-two dollars, an' now I is got only dis." Here he gave a loud laugh and said:

"Ole mule, I want you mighty bad, but I'll have to let you slide dis time."

While the large dealers were selling their products and emptying their wagons, those with vegetables and fruits were vending them in different sections of the city. A man with a large basket upon his head came along through one of the principal streets shouting:

"Hellow, dar, in de cellar, I is got fresh aggs, jess fum de hen, lay 'em dis mornin' fer de 'casion; here dey is, big hen's aggs, cheap. Now's yer time. Dees aggs is fresh an' good, an' will make fuss-rate agg-nog. Now's yer time fer agg-nogg wid new aggs in it; all laid dis mornin'." Here he set down his basket as if to rest his head. Seeing a colored servant at one of the windows, he called out:

"Here, sister, here's de fresh aggs; here dey is, big aggs fum big hen, much as she could do to lay 'em. Now's yer time; don't be foolish an' miss dis chance."

Just then, a man with a wagon-load of stuff came along, and his voice completely shut out the man with "de fresh aggs."

"Here," cried he, "here's yer nice winter squash, taters, — Irish taters, sweet taters, Carliner taters. Big House, dar, Big House, look out de winder; here's yer nice cabbages, taters, sweet taters, squash. Now's yer time to get 'em cheap. To-morrow is Christmas, an' yer'll want 'em, shore."

The man with the basket of eggs on his head, and who had been silenced by the overpowering voice of the "tater" man, called out to the other, "Now, I reckon yer better go in anudder street. I's been totin' dees aggs all day, an' I don't get in nobody's way."

"I want to know, is dis your street?" asked the "tater" man.

"No; but I tank de Lord, I is got some manners 'bout me. But, den, I couldn't speck no more fum you, fer I knowed you afore de war ; you was one of dem cheap niggers, clodhopper, never taste a bit of white bread till after de war, an' den didn't know 'twas bread."

"Well, den, ef you make so much fuss 'bout de street, I'll go out of it; it's nothin' but a second-handed street, no how," said the "tater" man, and drove off, crying, "taters, sweet taters, Irish taters, an' squash."

Passing into a street where the colored people are largely represented, I met another head peddler. This man had a tub on his head and with a musical voice was singing : —

> " Here's yer chitlins, fresh an' sweet,
>   Who'll jine de Union?

Young hog's chitlins hard to beat,
 Who'll jine de Union?
Methodist chitlins, jest been biled,
 Who'll jine de Union?
Right fresh chitlins, dey ain't spiled,
 Who'll jine de Union?
Baptist chitlins by de pound,
 Who'll jine de Union?
As nice chitlins as ever was found,
 Who'll jine de Union?

"Here's yer chitlins, out of good fat hog; jess as sweet chitlins as ever yer see. Dees chitlins will make yer mouf water jess to look at 'em. Come an' see 'em."

At this juncture the man took the tub from his head, sat it down, to answer a woman who had challenged his right to call them "Baptist chitlins."

"Duz you mean to say dat dem is Baptiss chitlins?"

"Yes, mum, I means to say dat dey is real Baptist chitlins, an' nuffin' else."

"Did dey come out of a Baptiss hog?" inquired the woman.

"Yes, mum, dem chitlins come out of a Baptist hog."

"How duz you make dat out?"

"Well, yer see, dat hog was raised by Mr. Rober-son, a hard-shell Baptist, de corn dat de hog was fatted on was also raised by Baptists, he was killed and dressed by Geemes Boone, an' you all know dat he'e as big a Baptist as ever lived."

"Well," said the woman, as if perfectly satisfied, "lem-me have two poun's."

By the time the man had finished his explanation, and weighed out her lot, he was completely surrounded with women and men, nearly all of whom had their dishes to get the choice morsel in.

"Now," said a rather solid-looking man. "Now, I want some of de Meth-diss chitlins dat you's bin talking 'bout."

"Here dey is, ser."

"What," asked the purchaser, "you take 'em all out of de same tub?"

"Yes," quickly replied the vender.

"Can you tell 'em by lookin' at 'em?" inquired the chubby man.

"Yes, ser."

"How duz you tell 'em?"

"Well, ser, de Baptist chitlins has bin more in de water, you see, an' dey's a little whiter."

"But, how duz I know dat dey is Meth-diss?"

"Well, ser, dat hog was raised by Uncle Jake Bemis, one of de most shoutin' Methodist in de Zion connection. Well, you see, ser, de hog pen was right close to de house, an' dat hog was so knowin' dat when Uncle Jake went to prayers, ef dat hog was squeelin' he'd stop. Why, ser, you could hardly get a grunt out of dat hog till Uncle Jake was dun his prayer. Now, ser, ef dat don't make him a Methodist hog, what will?"

"Weigh me out four pounds, ser."

"Here's your fresh chitlins, Baptist chitlins, Methodist chitlins, all good an' sweet."

And in an hour's time the peddler, with his empty

tub upon his head, was making his way out of the
street, singing, —

> " Methodist chitlins, Baptist chitlins,
>   Who'll jine de Union ? "

Hearing the colored cotton-growers were to have
a meeting that night, a few miles from the city, and
being invited to attend, I embraced the opportunity.
Some thirty persons were assembled, and as I entered the room, I heard them chanting —

> Sing yo' praises ! Bless de Lam!
>   Getting plenty money !
> Cotton's gwine up — 'deed it am !
>   People, ain't it funny?

CHORUS. — Rise, shine, give God the glory.
                                        [*Repeat* glory.]

> Don't you tink hit's gwine to rain?
>   Maybe was, a little ;
> Maybe one ole hurricane
>   'S bilin' in de kittle ! — *Chorus.*

> Craps done fail in Egypt lan' —
>   Say so in de papers ;
> Maybe little slight o' hand
>   'Mong de specerlaters. — *Chorus.*

> Put no faith in solemn views ;
>   Keep yo' pot a smokin',
> Stan' up squah in yo' own shoes —
>   Keep de debble chokin' ! — *Chorus.*

Fetch me 'roun' dat tater juice !
Stop dat sassy grinnin' !
Turn dat stopper clean a-loose —
Keep yo' eye a skinnin' ! — *Chorus.*

Here's good luck to Egypt lan' !
Hope she ain't a-failin' !
Hates to see my fellerman
Straddle ob de pailin' ! — *Chorus.*

The church filled up ; the meeting was well conducted, and measures taken to protect cotton-raisers,
showing that these people, newly-made free, and
uneducated, were looking to their interests.

Paying a flying visit to Tennessee, I halted at
Columbia, the capital of Maury County. At Redg-
erford Creek, five miles distant from Columbia, lives
Joe Budge, a man with one hundred children. Never
having met one with such a family, I resolved to
make a call on the gentleman and satisfy my own
curiosity.

This distinguished individual is seventy-one years
old, large frame, of unadulterated blood, and spent
his life in slavery up to the close of the war.

" How many children have you, Mr. Budge ? " I
asked.

" One hundred, ser," was the quick response.

" Are they all living ? "

" No, ser."

" How many wives had you ? "

" Thirteen, ser."

" Had you more than one wife living at any time ? "

"O, yes, ser, nearly all of dem ware livin' when de war broke out."

"How was this, did the law allow you to have more than one wife at a time?"

"Well, yer see, boss, I waren't under de law, I ware under marser."

"Were you married to all of your wives by a minister?"

"No, ser, only five by de preacher."

"How did you marry the others?"

"Ober de broomstick an' under de blanket."

"How was that performed?"

"Well, yer see, ser, dey all 'sembles in de quarters, an' a man takes hold of one en' of de broom an' a 'oman takes hole of tudder en', an' dey holes up de broom, an' de man an' de 'oman dats gwine to get married jumps ober an' den slips under a blanket, dey put out de light an' all goes out an' leabs em dar."

"How near together were your wives?"

"Marser had fore plantations, an' dey live 'bout on 'em, dem dat warn't sold."

"Did your master sell some of your wives?"

"O! yes, ser, when dey got too ole to bare children. You see, marser raised slaves fer de market, an' my stock ware called mighty good, kase I ware very strong, an' could do a heap of work."

"Were your children sold away from you?"

"Yes, ser, I see three of 'em sole one day fer two thousand dollars a-piece; yer see dey ware men grown up."

"Did you select your wives?"

"Dunno what you mean by dat word."

"Did you pick out the women that you wanted?"

"O! no, ser, I had nuthin ter say 'bout dat. Marser allers get 'em, an' pick out strong, hearty young women. Dat's de reason dat de planters wanted to get my children, kase dey ware so helty."

"Did you never feel that it was wrong to get married in such a light manner?"

"No, ser, kase yer see I toted de witness wid me."

"What do you mean by that?"

"Why, ser, I had religion, an' dat made me feel dat all ware right."

"What was the witness that you spoke of?"

"De change of heart, ser, is de witness dat I totes in my bosom; an' when a man's got dat, he fears nuthin, not eben de debble himsef."

"Then you know that you've got the witness?"

"Yes, ser, I totes it right here." And at this point, Mr. Budge put his hand on his heart, and looked up to heaven.

"I presume your master made no profession of religion?"

"O! yes, ser, you bet he had religion. He ware de fustest man in de church, an' he ware called mighty powerful in prayer."

"Do any of your wives live near you now, except the one that you are living with?"

"Yes, ser, dar's five in dis county, but dey's all married now to udder men."

"Have you many grand-children?"

" Yes, ser, when my 'lations am all tergedder, dey numbers 'bout fore hundred, near as I ken get at it."

" Do you know of any other men that have got as many children as you?"

" No, ser, dey calls me de boss daddy in dis part of de State."

Having satisfied my curiosity, I bade Mr. Budge "good-day."

CHAPTER XIX.

SPENDING part of the winter of 1880 in Tennessee, I began the study of the character of the people and their institutions. I soon learned that there existed an intense hatred on the part of the whites, toward the colored population. Looking at the past, this was easily accounted for. The older whites, brought up in the lap of luxury, educated to believe themselves superior to the race under them, self-willed, arrogant, determined, skilled in the use of side-arms, wealthy — possessing the entire political control of the State — feeling themselves superior also to the citizens of the free States, — this people was called upon to subjugate themselves to an ignorant, superstitious, and poverty-stricken, race — a race without homes, or the means of obtaining them; to see the offices of State filled by men

selected from this servile set made these whites feel
themselves deeply degraded in the eyes of the world.
Their power was gone, but their pride still remained.
They submitted in silence, but "bided their time,"
and said: "Never mind; we'll yet make your hell a
hot one."

The blacks felt their importance, saw their own
power in national politics, were interviewed by obsequious and cringing white men from the North —
men, many of them, far inferior, morally, to the
negro. Two-faced, second-class white men of the
South, few in number, it is true, hung like leeches
upon the blacks. Among the latter was a respectable
proportion of free men — free before the Rebellion;
these were comparatively well educated; to these
and to the better class of freedmen the country was
to look for solid work. In the different State Legislatures, the great battle was to be fought, and to
these the interest of the South centred. All of the
Legislatures were composed mainly of colored men.
The few whites that were there were not only no
help to the blacks, but it would have been better for
the character of the latter, and for the country at large,
if most of them had been in some State prison.

Colored men went into the Legislatures somewhat
as children go for the first time to a Sabbath school.
They sat and waited to see "the show." Many had
been elected by constituencies, of which not more
than ten in a hundred could read the ballots they
deposited; and a large number of these Representatives could not write their own names.

This was not their fault. Their want of education was attributable to the system of slavery through which they had passed, and the absence of the educated intelligent whites of the South, was not the fault of the colored men. This was a trying position for the recently-enfranchised blacks, but nobly did they rise above the circumstances. The speeches made by some of these men exhibited a depth of thought, flights of eloquence, and civilized statesmanship, that throw their former masters far in the back-ground. Yet, amongst the good done, bills were introduced and passed, giving State aid to unworthy objects, old, worn-out corporations re-galvanized, bills for outrageous new frauds drawn up by white men, and presented by blacks; votes of both colors bought up, bills passed, money granted, and these ignorant men congratulated as "Statesmen."

While this "Comedy of Errors" was being performed at the South, and loudly applauded at the North, these very Northern men, who had yelled their throats sore, would have fainted at the idea of a negro being elected a member of their own Legislature.

By and by came the reaction. The disfranchised whites of the South submitted, but complained. Northern men and women, the latter, always the most influential, sympathized with the dog underneath. As the tide was turning, the white adventurers returned from the South with piles of greenbacks, and said that they had been speculating in cotton; but their neighbors knew that it was stolen, for they had been members of Southern Legislatures.

While Northern carpet-baggers were scudding off to their kennels with their ill-gotten gains, the Southern colored politicians were driving fast horses, their wives in their fine carriages; and men, who, five years before were working in the cotton field under the lash, could now draw their checks for thousands.

This extravagance of black men, followed by the heavy taxes, reminded the old Southerners of their defeat in the Rebellion; it brought up thoughts of revenge; Northern sympathy emboldened them at the South, which resulted in the Ku-Klux organizations, and the reign of terror that has cursed the South ever since.

The restoring of the rebels to power and the surrendering the colored people to them, after using the latter in the war, and at the ballot box, creating an emnity between the races, is the most bare-faced ingratitude that history gives any account of.

After all, the ten years of negro ˙Legislation in the South challenges the profoundest study of mankind. History does not record a similar instance. Five millions of uneducated, degraded people, without any preparation whatever, set at liberty in a single day, without shedding a drop of blood, burning a barn, or insulting a single female. They reconstructed the State Governments that their masters had destroyed; became Legislators, held

State offices, and with all their blunders, surpassed the whites that had preceded them. Future generations will marvel at the calm forbearance, good sense, and Christian zeal of the American Negro of the nineteenth century.

Nothing has been left undone to cripple their energies, darken their minds, debase their moral sense, and obliterate all traces of their relationship to the rest of mankind; and yet how wonderfully they have sustained the mighty load of oppression under which they have groaned for thousands of years.

After looking at the past history of both races, I could easily see the cause of the great antipathy of the white man to the black, here in Tennessee. This feeling was most forcibly illustrated by an incident that occurred one day while I was standing in front of the Knoxville House, in Knoxville. A good-looking, well-dressed colored man approached a white man, in a business-like manner, and began talking to him, but ere he had finished the question, the white raised his walking stick, and with much force, knocked off the black man's hat, and with an oath said, "Don't you know better than to speak to a white man with your hat on, where's your manners?" The negro picked up his hat, held it in his hand, and resumed the conversation.

I inquired of the colored gentleman with whom I was talking, who the parties were; he replied, — " The white man is a real estate dealer, and the colored man is Hon. Mr. ——, ex-member of the General Assembly."

This race feeling is still more forcibly set forth in the dastardly attack of John Warren, of Huntingdon. The wife of this ruffian, while passing through one of the streets of that town, was accidentally run against by Miss Florence Hayes, who offered ample apology, and which would have been accepted by any well-bred lady. However, Mrs. Warren would not be satisfied with anything less than the punishment of the young lady. Therefore, the two-fisted, coarse, rough, uncouth ex-slave-holder, proceeded to Miss Hayes' residence, gained admission, and without a word of ceremony seized the young lady by the hair, and began beating her with his fist, and kicking her with his heavy boots.

Not until his victim lay prostrate and senseless at his feet, did this fiend cease his blows. Miss Hayes was teaching school at Huntingdon when this outrage was committed, and so severe was the barbarous attack, that she was compelled to return to her home at Nashville, where she was confined to her room for several weeks. Yet, neither law nor public opinion could reach this monster.

A few days after the assault, the following paragraph appeared in the Huntingdon *Vindicator:*

"The occurrences of the past two weeks in the town of Huntingdon should prove conclusively to the colored citizens that there is a certain line existing between themselves and the white people which they cannot cross with impunity. The incident which prompts us to write this article, is the thrashing which a white gentleman administered to a colored woman last week. With no wish to foster a spirit of lawlessness in this community, but actuated by a desire to see the negro keep in his proper place, we advise white men everywhere to *stand up for their rights*, and in no case yield an inch to the encroachment of an inferior race."

"Stand up for their rights," with this editor, means for the white ruffianly coward to knock down every colored lady that does not give up the entire sidewalk to him or his wife.

It was my good fortune to meet on several occasions Miss Florence T. Hayes, the young lady above alluded to, and I never came in contact with a more retiring, lady-like person in my life. She is a student of Tennessee Central College, where she bears an unstained reputation, and is regarded by all who know her to possess intellectual gifts far superior to the average white young women of Tennessee.

Spending a night in the country, we had just risen from the supper-table when mine host said :

"Listen, Mingo is telling how he re-converted his daughter ; listen, you'll hear a rich story, and a true one." Mr. Mingo lived in the adjoining room.

"Yes, Mrs. Jones, my darter has bin home wissitin' me, an' I had a mighty trial wid her, I can tell yer."

"What was the matter, Mr. Mingo?" inquired the visitor.

"Well, yer see, Fanny's bin a-livin' in Philamadelfy, an' she's a mighty changed 'oman in her ways.

When she come in de house, she run up to her
mammy and say, — 'O! mar, I'm exquisitely pleased
to greet you.' Den she run ter me an' sed, — 'O!
par,' an' kiss me. Well, dat was all well enuff, but
to see as much as two yards of her dress a-dragin'
behind her on de floor, it was too much, — an' it were
silk, too. It made my heart ache. Ses I, — 'Fanny,
you's very stravagant, dragin' all dat silk on de floor
in dat way.' 'O!' sed she, 'that's the fashion,
par.' Den, yer see, I were uneasy fer her. I were
'fraid she'd fall, fer she had on a pair of boots wid
the highess heels I eber see in my life, which made
her walk as ef she were walkin' on her toes. Den,
she were covered all over wid ribbons and ruffles.

"When we set down to dinner, Fanny eat wid her
fork, an' when she see her sister put de knife in her
mouf, she ses, — 'Don't put your knife in your
mouth; that's vulgar.' Nex' mornin', she took out
of her pocket some seeds, an' put 'em in a tin cup,
an' pour bilin' hot water on 'em. Ses I, — 'Fanny,
is yer sick, an' gwine to take some medicine?'

"'O! no, par, it's quince seed, to make some
gum-stick-um.'

"'What is dat fer?' I axed.

"'Why, par, it's to make Grecian waves on my
forehead. Some call them "scallopes." We ladies
in the city make them. You see, par, we comb our
hair down in little waves, and the gum makes them
stick close to the forehead. All the white ladies in
the city wear them; it's all the fashion.'

"Well, yer see, Mrs. Jones, I could stand all dat,

but when we went to prayers I ax Fanny to lead in
prayer; an' when dat gal got on her knees and took
out of her pocket a gilt-edge book, and read a
prayer, den I were done, I ax myself is it possible
dat my darter is come to dat. So, when prayer
were over, I sed : 'Fanny, what kind of religion is
dat yer's got?' Sed she,—'Why, par, I em a
Piscopion.' 'What is dat?' I axed. 'That's the
English Church service. Den yer's no more a
Methodist?' 'O! no,' said she, 'to be a Piscopion
is all the fashion.'"

"Stop, Mr. Mingo," sed Mrs. Jones; "what kind
of religion is dat? Is it Baptiss?"

"No, no," replied the old man; "ef it were Baptiss, den I could a-stood dat, kase de Baptiss religion
will do when yer can't get no better. Fer wid all
dey faults, I believe de Baptiss ken get into hebben
by a tight squeeze. Kase, yer see, Mrs. Jones, I is
a Methodiss, an' I believes in ole-time religion, an' I
wants my chillen to meet me in hebben. So, I jess
went right down on my knees an' ax de Lord to
show me my juty about Fanny, fer I wanted to win
her back to de ole-time religion. Well, de Lord
made it all plain to me, an' follerin' de Lord's message to me, I got right up an' went out into de
woods an' cut some switches, an' put 'em in de barn.
So I sed to Fanny : 'Come, my darter, but to de
barn; I want to give yer a present to take back to
Philamadelfy wid yer.'

"'Yes, par,' said she, fer she was a-fixin' de 'gum-
stick-um' on her hair. So I went to de barn, an'

very soon out come Fanny. I jess shut de door an'
fasten it, and took down my switches, an' ax her, —
'What kind of religion is dat yer's got?'

"'Piscopion, par.' Den I commence, an' I did
give dat gal sech a whippen, and she cry out, — 'O!
par. O! par, please stop, par.' Den I ax her, —
'What kind of religion yer's got?' 'Pis-co-copion,'
sed she. So I give her some moo, an' I ax her
again, — 'What kind of religion is yer got?' She
sed, — 'O! par, O! par.' Sed I, — 'Don't call me
"par." Call me in de right way.' Den she said, —
'O! daddy, O! daddy, I is a Methodiss. I is got
ole-time religion; please stop an' I'll never be a
Piscopion any more.'

"So, yer see, Mrs. Jones, I converted dat gal right
back to de ole-time religion, which is de bess of all
religion. Yes, de Lord answered my prayer dat
time, wid de aid of de switches."

Whether Mingo's conversion of his daughter kept
her from joining the Episcopalians, on her return to
Philadelphia, or not, I have not learned.

CHAPTER XX.

THE moral and social degradation of the colored population of the Southern States, is
attributable to two main causes, their mode of
living, and their religion. In treating upon these

causes, and especially the latter, I feel confident
that I shall throw myself open to the criticism of a
numerous, if not an intelligent class of the people
upon whom I write.   The entire absence of a
knowledge of the laws of physiology, amongst the
colored inhabitants of the South is proverbial.
Their small unventilated houses, in poor streets and
dark alleys, in cities and towns, and the poorly-
built log huts in the country, are often not fit for
horses.   A room fifteen feet square, with two, and
sometimes three beds, and three or four in a bed, is
common in Tennessee.

No bathing conveniences whatever, and often not
a wash dish about the house, is the rule.   The most
inveterate eaters in the world, yet these people have
no idea of cooking outside of hog, hominy, corn
bread, and coffee.   Yes, there is one more dish, it
is the negro's sun-flower in the South, cabbages.

It is usual to see a woman coming from the
market about five o'clock in the evening, with a
basket under her shawl, and in it a piece of pork,
bacon, or half a hog's head, and one or two large
heads of cabbage, and some sweet potatoes.   These
are put to cook at once, and the odor from the boiling pot may be snuffed in some distance off.

Generous to a fault, the host invites all who call
in, to "stop to supper."   They sit down to the
table at about nine o'clock, spend fully an hour over
the first course, then the apple dumplings, after
that, the coffee and cake.   Very few vegetables,
except cabbages and sweet potatoes, are ever used

by these people. Consequently they are not unfrequently ill from a want of the knowledge of the laws of health. The assembling of large numbers in the cities and towns has proved fatal.

Nearly all the statistics relating to the subject now accessible are those coming from the larger Southern cities, and these would seem to leave no doubt that in such centres of population the mortality of the colored greatly exceeds that of the white race. In Washington, for instance, where the negroes have enjoyed longer and more privileges than in most Southern cities, the death-rate per thousand in the year 1876 was for the whites 26.537; for the colored 49.294; and for the previous year it was a little worse for the blacks. In Baltimore, a very healthy city, the total death-rate for 1875 was 21.67 in one thousand, of which the whites showed 19.80, the colored 34.42. In a still healthier little city, Chattanooga, Tenn., the statistics of the last five years give the death-rate of the whites at 19.9; of the colored, 37. The very best showing for the latter, singularly enough, is made in Selma, Ala. It stands per one thousand, white, 14.28; colored, 18.88. In Mobile, in the same State, the mortality of the colored was just about double the rate among the whites. New Orleans for 1875 gives the record of 25.45 for the death-rate of the whites, to 39.69 for that of the colored.

Lecturers of their own race, male and female, upon the laws of health, is the first move needed.

After settling the question with his bacon and

cabbage, the next dearest thing to a colored man, in the South, is his religion. I call it a "thing," because they always speak of getting religion as if they were going to market for it.

"You better go an' get religion, dat's what you better do, fer de devil will be arter you one of dees days, and den whar will yer be?" said an elderly Sister, who was on her way to the "Revival," at St. Paul's, in Nashville, last winter. The man to whom she addressed these words of advice stopped, raised his hat, and replied:

"Anty, I ain't quite ready to-night, but I em gwine to get it before the meetins close, kase when that getting-up day comes, I want to have the witness; that I do."

"Yes, yer better, fer ef yer don't, dar'll be a mighty stir 'mong de brimstone down dar, dat dey will, fer yer's bin bad nuff; I knows yer fum A to izzard," returned the old lady.

The church was already well filled, and the minister had taken his text. As the speaker warmed up in his subject, the Sisters began to swing their heads and reel to and fro, and eventually began a shout. Soon, five or six were fairly at it, which threw the house into a buzz. Seats were soon vacated near the shouters, to give them more room, because the women did not wish to have their hats smashed in by the frenzied Sisters. As a woman sprung up in her seat, throwing up her long arms, with a loud scream, the lady on the adjoining seat quickly left, and did not stop till she got to a safe distance.

"Ah, ha!" exclaimed a woman near by, "'fraid of your new bonnet! Ain't got much religion, I reckon. Specks you'll have to come out of that if you want to save your soul."

"She thinks more of that hat now, than she does of a seat in heaven," said another.

"Never mind," said a third, "when she gets de witness, she'll drap dat hat an' shout herself out of breath."

The shouting now became general; a dozen or more entering into it most heartily. These demonstrations increased or abated, according to movements of the leaders, who were in and about the pulpit; for the minister had closed his discourse, and first one, and then another would engage in prayer. The meeting was kept up till a late hour, during which, four or five sisters becoming exhausted, had fallen upon the floor and lay there, or had been removed by their friends.

St. Paul is a fine structure, with its spire bathed in the clouds, and standing on the rising land in South Cherry Street, it is a building that the citizens may well be proud of.

In the evening I went to the First Baptist Church, in Spruce Street. This house is equal in size and finish to St. Paul. A large assembly was in attendance, and a young man from Cincinnati was introduced by the pastor as the preacher for the time being. He evidently felt that to set a congregation to shouting, was the highest point to be attained, and he was equal to the occasion. Failing to raise a good shout by a reasonable amount of exertion, he took from his pocket a letter, opened it, held it up and began, "When you reach the other world you'll be hunting for your mother, and the angel will read from this paper. Yes, the angel will read from this paper."

For fully ten minutes the preacher walked the pulpit, repeating in a loud, incoherent manner, "And the angel will read from this letter." This created the wildest excitement, and not less than ten or fifteen were shouting in different parts of the house, while four or five were going from seat to seat shaking hands with the occupants of the pews. "Let dat angel come right down now an' read dat letter," shouted a Sister, at the top of her voice. This was the signal for loud exclamations from various parts of the house. "Yes, yes, I want's to hear the letter." "Come, Jesus, come, or send an angel to read the letter." "Lord, send us the power." And other remarks filled the house. The pastor highly complimented the effort, as one of "great power," which the audience most cordially endorsed. At the close of the service the strange minister had hearty shakes of the hand from a large number of leading men and women of the church. And this was one of the most refined congregations in Nashville.

It will be difficult to erase from the mind of the negro of the South, the prevailing idea that outward demonstrations, such as, shouting, the loud "amen," and the most boisterous noise in prayer, are not necessary adjuncts to piety.

A young lady of good education and refinement, residing in East Tennessee, told me that she had joined the church about a year previous, and not until she had one shouting spell, did most of her Sisters believe that she had "the Witness."

"And did you really shout?" I inquired.

"Yes. I did it to stop their mouths, for at nearly every meeting, one or more would say, 'Sister Smith, I hope to live to see you show that you've got the Witness, for where the grace of God is, there will be shouting, and the sooner you comes to that point the better it will be for you in the world to come.'"

To get religion, join a benevolent society that will pay them "sick dues" when they are ill, and to bury them when they die, appears to be the beginning, the aim, and the end of the desires of the colored people of the South. In Petersburg I was informed that there were thirty-two different secret societies in that city, and I met persons who held membership in four at the same time. While such associations are of great benefit to the improvident, they are, upon the whole, very injurious. They take away all stimulus to secure homes and to provide for the future.

As a man observed to me, "I b'longs ter four s'ieties, de 'Samaritans,' de 'Gallalean Fisherman,' de 'Sons of Moses,' an' de 'Wise Men of de East.' All of dees pays me two dollars a week when I is sick, an' twenty-five dollars ter bury me when I dies. Now ain't dat good?"

I replied that I thought it would be far better, if he put his money in a home and educated himself."

"Well," said he, "I is satisfied, kas, ef I put de money in a house, maybe when I got sick some udder man might be hangin' roun' wantin' me ter die, an' maybe de ole 'oman might want me gone too, an' not take good kere of me, an' let me die an' let de town bury me. But, now, yer see, de s'iety takes kere of me and burries me. So, now, I am all right fer dis worl' an' I is got de Witness, an' dat fixes me fer hebben."

This was all said in an earnest manner, showing that the brother had an eye to business.

The determination of late years to ape the whites in the erection of costly structures to worship in, is very injurious to our people. In Petersburg, Va., a Baptist society pulled down a noble building, which was of ample size, to give place to a more fashionable and expensive one, simply because a sister Church had surpassed them in putting up a house of worship. It is more consistent with piety and Godly sincerity to say that we don't believe there is any soul-saving and God-honoring element in such expensive and useless ornaments to houses in which to meet and humbly worship in simplicity and sincerity the true and living God, according to his revealed will. Poor, laboring people who are without homes of their own, and without (in many instances) steady remunerative employment, can ill afford to pay high for useless and showy things that neither instruct nor edify them. The manner, too, in which the money is raised, is none of the best, to say the least of it. For most of the money, both to build the churches

and to pay the ministers, is the hard earnings of men
in the fields, at service, or by our women over the
wash-tub. When our people met and worshipped
in less costly and ornamental houses, their piety and
sincerity was equally as good as now, if not better.
With more polish within and less ornament without,
we would be more spiritually and less worldly-
minded.

Revival meetings, and the lateness of the hours at
which they close, are injurious to both health and
morals. Many of the churches begin in October,
and continue till the holidays; and commencing
again the middle of January, they close in April.
They often keep the meetings in till eleven o'clock;
sometimes till twelve; and in some country places,
they have gone on later. I was informed of a young
woman who lost her situation — a very good one —
because the family could not sit up till twelve o'clock
every night to let her in, and she would not leave her
meeting so as to return earlier. Another source of
moral degradation lies in the fact that a very large
number of men, calling themselves "missionaries,"
travel the length and breadth of the country, stopping
longest where they are best treated. The "missionary"
is usually armed with a recommendation from some
minister in charge, or has a forged one, it makes
but little difference which. He may be able to read
enough to line a hymn, but that is about all.

His paper that he carries speaks of him as a man
"gifted in revival efforts," and he at once sets about
getting up a revival meeting. This tramp, for he

cannot be called anything else, has with him generally a hymn-book, and an old faded, worn-out car-
pet-bag, with little or nothing in it. He remains in
a place just as long as the people will keep him,
which usually depends upon his ability to keep up
an excitement. I met a swarm of these lazy fellows
all over the South, the greatest number, however, in
West Virginia.

The only remedy for this great evil lies in an educated ministry, which is being supplied to a limited
extent. It is very difficult, however, to induce the
uneducated, superstitious masses to receive and support an intelligent Christian clergyman.

The great interest felt in the South for education
amongst the colored people often produce scenes of
humor peculiar to the race. Enjoying the hospi-
tality of a family in West Virginia, I was not a little
amused at the preparation made for the reception of
their eldest son, who had been absent six months at
Wilberforce College. A dinner with a turkey,
goose, pair of fowls, with a plentiful supply of side
dishes, and apple dumplings for dessert, was on the
table at the hour that the son was expected from the
train.

An accident delayed the cars to such an extent
that we were at the table and dinner half through,
when suddenly the door flew open, and before us
stood the hope of the family. The mother sprang
up, raised her hands and exclaimed, "Well, well, ef
dar ain't Peter, now. De Lord bress dat chile, eh,
an' how college-like he seems. Jess look at him,

don't he look edecated? Come right here dis minit
an' kiss your mammy."

During this pleasant greeting, Peter stood near
the door where he had entered; dressed in his
college rig, small cap on his head, bag swung at his
side, umbrella in the left hand, and a cigar in the
right, with a smile on his countenance, he looked
the very personification of the Harvard student.
The father of the family, still holding his knife and
fork, sat with a glow upon his face, while the two
youngsters, taking advantage of the occasion, were
helping themselves to the eatables.

At the bidding, "Come an' kiss your mammy,"
Peter came forward and did the nice thing to all
except the youngest boy, who said, "I can't kiss yer
now, Pete, wait till I eat dees dumplins, den I'll kiss
yer."

Dinner over, and Peter gave us some humorous
accounts of college life, to the great delight of his
mother, who would occasionally exclaim, "Bress de
chile, what a hard time he muss hab dar at de college.
An' how dem boys wory's him. Well, people's got
to undergo a heap to git book larnin', don't dey?"

At night the house was filled, to see the young
man from college.

CHAPTER XXI.

IN the olden time, ere a blow was struck in the
Rebellion, the whites of the South did the think-

ing, and the blacks did the work; the master planned, and the slave executed. This unfitted both for the new dispensation that was fast coming, and left each helpless, without the other.

But the negro was the worst off of the two, for he had nothing but his hands, while tne white man had his education, backed up by the lands that he owned. Who can wonder at the negro's improvidence and his shiftlessness, when he has never had any systematic training — never been compelled to meet the cares of life?

This was the black man's misfortune on gaining his freedom, and to learn to save, and to manage his own affairs, appeared to all to be his first duty.

The hope of every one, therefore, seemed to centre in the Freedman's Saving Bank. "This is our bank," said they; and to this institution the intelligent and the ignorant, the soldier fresh from the field of battle, the farmer, the day laborer, and the poor washerwoman, all alike brought their earnings and deposited them in the Freedman's Bank. This place of safety for their scanty store seemed to be the hope of the race for the future. It was a stimulus for a people who had never before been permitted to enter a moneyed institution, except at his master's heels, to bring or to take away the bag of silver that his owner was too proud or too lazy to "tote."

So great was the negro's wish to save, that the deposits in the Freedman's Bank increased from three hundred thousand dollars, in 1866, to thirty-one million dollars, in 1872, and to fifty-five million dollars, in 1874. This saving of earnings became infectious throughout the South, and the family that had no bank-book was considered poorly off. These deposits were the first instalments toward purchasing homes, or getting ready to begin some mercantile or mechanical business. The first announcement, therefore, of the closing of the Freedman's Saving Bank had a paralyzing effect upon the blacks everywhere.

Large numbers quit work; the greater portion sold their bank-books for a trifle, and general distrust prevailed throughout the community. Many who had purchased small farms, or cheap dwellings in cities and towns, and had paid part of the purchase money, now became discouraged, surrendered their claims, gave up the lands, and went about as if every hope was lost. It was their first and their last dealings with a bank.

These poor people received no sympathy whatever, from the whites of the South. Indeed, the latter felt to rejoice, for the negro obtained his liberty through the Republican party, and the Freedmen's Bank was a pet of that party.

The negro is an industrious creature, laziness is not his chief fault, and those who had left their work, returned to it. But the charm for saving was gone.

"No more Banks for me, I'll use my money as I get it, and then I'll know where it has gone to," said an intelligent and well-informed colored man to me.

This want of confidence in the saving institutions

of the country, has caused a gener.l spending of money as soon as obtained ; and railroad excursions, steamboat rides, hiring of horses and buggies on Sabbath, and even on week days, have reaped large sums from colored people all over the South. Verily, the failure of the Freedman's Saving Bank was a National calamity, the influence of which will be felt for many years.

Not satisfied with robbing the deluded people out of the bulk of their hard earnings, commissioners were appointed soon after the failure, with "appropriate" salaries, to look after the interest of the depositors, and these leeches are eating up the remainder.

Whether truly or falsely, the freedmen were led to believe that the United States Government was responsible to them for the return of their money with interest. Common justice would seem to call for some action in the matter.

CHAPTER XXII.

THOSE who recollect the standing of Virginia in days gone by, will be disappointed in her at the present time. The people, both white and black, are poor and proud, all living on their reputation when the "Old Dominion" was considered the first State in the Union.

I viewed Richmond with much interest. The effect of the late Rebellion is still visible everywhere,

and especially amongst those who were leaders in
society thirty years ago.   I walked through the
market and observed several men with long, black
cloth cloaks, beneath which was a basket.   Into this
they might be seen to deposit their marketing for
the day.

I noticed an old black man bowing very gracefully
to one of these individuals, and I inquired who he
was.   "Ah, massa," said the negro, "dat is Major
——, he was berry rich before de war, but de war
fotch him right down, and now he ain't able to have
servants, and he's too proud to show his basket, so
he covers it up in his cloak."   And then the black
man smiled and shook his head significantly, and
walked on.   Stánding here in the market place, one
beholds many scenes which bring up the days of
slavery as seen by the results.   Here is a girl with
a rich brown skin; after her comes one upon whose
cheek a blush can just be distinguished; and I saw
one or two young women whose cream-like complexion would have justly excited the envy of many a
New York belle.   The condition of the women of
the latter class is most deplorable.   Beautiful almost
beyond description, many of them educated and
refined, with the best white blood of the South in
their veins, it is perhaps only natural that they
should refuse to mate themselves with coarse and
ignorant black men.   Socially, they are not recognized by the whites; they are often without money
enough to buy the barest necessaries of life; honor-
ably they can never procure sufficient means to

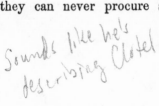

gratify their luxurious tastes; their mothers have *a la Curser*
taught them how to sin; their fathers they never
knew; debauched white men are ever ready to take
advantage of their destitution, and after living a
short life of shame and dishonor they sink into early
and unhallowed graves. Living, they were despised
by whites and blacks alike; dead, they are mourned
by none.

I went to hear the somewhat celebrated negro
preacher, Rev. John Jasper. The occasion was one
of considerable note, he having preached, and by
request, a sermon to prove that the "Sun do move,"
and now he was to give it at the solicitation of
forty-five members of the Legislature, who were
present as hearers.

Those who wanted the sermon repeated were all
whites, a number of whom did it for the fun that
they expected to enjoy, while quite a respectable
portion, old fogy in opinion, felt that the preacher
was right.

On reaching the church, I found twelve carriages
and two omnibuses, besides a number of smaller
vehicles, lining the street, half an hour before the
opening of the doors. However, the whites who
had come in these conveyances had been admitted
by the side doors, while the streets were crowded
with blacks and a poorer class of whites.

By special favor I was permitted to enter before
the throng came rushing in. Members of the Legislature were assigned the best seats, indeed, the entire
centre of the house was occupied by whites, who,

I was informed, were from amongst the F. F. Vs.
The church seats one thousand, but it is safe to say
that twelve hundred were present at that time.

Rev. John Jasper is a deep black, tall, and slim,
with long arms and somewhat round-shouldered, and
sixty-five years old. He has preached in Richmond
for the last forty-five years, and is considered a very
good man. He is a fluent speaker, well versed in
Scriptures, and possesses a large amount of wit. The
members of Jasper's church are mainly freedmen, a
large number of whom are from the country, commonly called "corn-field niggers."

The more educated class of the colored people, I
found, did not patronize Jasper. They consider
him behind the times, and called him "old fogy."
Jasper looked proudly upon his audience, and well
he might, for he had before him some of the first
men and women of Virginia's capital. But these
people had not come to be instructed, they had
really come for a good laugh and were not disappointed.

Jasper had prepared for the occasion, and in his
opening service saved himself by calling on "Brother
Scogin" to offer prayer. This venerable Brother
evidently felt the weight of responsibility laid upon
him, and discharged the duty, at least to the entire
satisfaction of those who were there to be amused.
After making a very sensible prayer, Scogin concluded as follows : — "O Lord, we's a mighty abused
people, we's had a hard time in slavery, we's been
all broken to pieces, we's bow-legged, knock-kneed,

bandy-shanked, cross-eyed, and a great many of us is hump-backed. Now, Lord, we wants to be mendid up, an' we wants you to come an' do it. Don't send an angel, for dis is too big a job for an angel. You made us, O Lord, an' you know our wants, an' you can fix us up as nobody else can. Come right down yourself, and come quickly." At this sentence Jasper gave a loud groan, and Scogin ceased. After service was over I was informed that when Jasper finds any of his members a little too long-winded in prayer, singing, or speaking, he gives that significant groan, which they all well understand. It means "enough."

The church was now completely jammed, and it was said that two thousand people sought admission in vain. Jasper's text was "God is a God of War." The preacher, though wrong in his conclusions, was happy in his quotations, fresh in his memory, and eloquently impressed his views upon his hearers.

He said, "If the sun does not move, why did Joshua command it to 'stand still?' Was Joshua wrong? If so, I had rather be wrong with Joshua than to be right with the modern philosophers. If this earth moves, the chimneys would be falling, tumbling in upon the roofs of the houses, the mountains and hills would be changing and levelling down, the rivers would be emptying out. You and I would be standing on our heads. Look at that mountain standing out yonder; it stood there fifty years ago when I was a boy. Would it be standing there if the earth was running round as they tell us?"

"No, blessed God," cried a Sister. Then the laugh came, and Jasper stood a moment with his arms folded. He continued : "The sun rises in the east and sets in the west ; do you think any one can make me believe that the earth can run around the world in a single day so as to give the sun a chance to set in the west?"

"No, siree, that doctrine don't go down with Jasper."

At this point the preacher paused for breath, and I heard an elderly white in an adjoining pew, say, in a somewhat solemn tone—"Jasper is right, the sun moves."

Taking up his bandanna, and wiping away the copious perspiration that flowed down his dusky cheeks, the preacher opened a note which had just been laid upon the desk, read it, and continued, —"A question is here asked me, and one that I am glad to answer, because a large number of my people, as well as others, can't see how the children of Israel were able to cross the Red Sea in safety, while Pharaoh and his hosts were drowned. I have told you again and again that everything was possible with God. But that don't seem to satisfy you.

"Those who doubt these things that you read in Holy Writ are like the infidel, — won't believe unless you can see the cause. Well, let me tell you. The infidel says that when the children of Israel crossed the Red Sea, it was in winter, and the sea was frozen over. This is a mistake, or· an intentional misrepresentation." Here the preacher gave vivid accounts of the sufferings and flight of the children of Israel, whose case he likened to the colored people of the South. The preacher wound up with an eloquent appeal to his congregation not to be led astray by "these new-fangled notions."

Great excitement is just now taking hold of the people upon the seeming interest that the colored inhabitants are manifesting in the Catholic religion. The Cathedral in Richmond is thrown open every Sunday evening to the blacks, when the bishop himself preaches to them, and it is not strange that the eloquent and persuasive voice of Bishop Kean, who says to the negro, "My dear beloved brethren," should captivate these despised people. ·I attended a meeting at the large African Baptist Church, where the Rev. Moses D. Hoge, D. D., was to preach to the colored people against Catholicism. Dr. Hoge, though noted for his eloquence, and terribly in earnest, could not rise higher in his appeals to the blacks than to say "men and women" to them.

The contrast was noticeable to all. After hearing Dr. Hoge through I asked an intelligent colored man how he liked his sermon. His reply was : "If Dr. Hoge is in earnest, why don't he open his own church and invite us in and preach to us there? Before he can make any impression on us, he must go to the Catholic Church and learn the spirit of brotherly love."

One Sunday, Bishop Kean said to the colored congregation, numbering twelve hundred, who had come to hear him : "There are distinctions in the

business and in the social world, but there are no
distinctions in the spiritual.   A soul is a soul before
God, may it be a black or a white man's.   God is no
respecter of persons, the Christian Church cannot
afford to be. The people who would not let you
learn to read before the war, are the ones now that
accuse me of trying to use you for political purposes.

"Now, my dear beloved brethren, when I attempt
to tell you how to vote, you need not come to hear
me preach any more."

The blacks have been so badly treated in the past
that kind words and social recognition will do much
to win them in the future, for success will not depend
so much upon their matter as upon their manner;
not so much upon their faith as upon the more
potent direct influence of their practice.   In this the
Catholics of the South have the inside track, for the
prejudice of the Protestants seems in a fair way to
let the negro go anywhere except to heaven, if they
have to go the same way.

CHAPTER XXIII.

NORFOLK is the place above all others, where
the "old-Verginny-never-tire" colored people
of the olden time may be found in their purity.
Here nearly everybody lives out of doors in the

warm weather.   This is not confined to the blacks.
On the sidewalks, in front of the best hotels, under
the awnings at store-doors, on the door-sills of private houses, and on the curbstones in the streets,
may be seen people of all classes.   But the blacks
especially give the inside of the house a wide berth
in the summer.

I went to the market, for I always like to visit the
markets on Saturday, for there you see "life among
the lowly," as you see it nowhere else.   Colored
men and women have a respectable number of stalls
in the Norfolk market, the management of which
does them great credit.

But the costermongers, or street-venders, are the
men of music.   "Here's yer nice vegables — green
corn, butter beans, taters, Irish taters, new, jess bin
digged ; come an' get 'em while dey is fresh.   Now's
yer time ; squash, Calafony quash, bess in de worl' ;
come an' git 'em now ; it'll be Sunday termorrer, an'
I'll be gone to church.   Big fat Mexican peas,
marrer fat squash, Protestant squash, good Catholic
vegables of all kinds."

> Now's yer time to git snap-beans,
> Okra, tomatoes, an' taters gwine by ;
> Don't be foolish virgins ;
> Hab de dinner ready
> When de master he comes home,
> Snap-beans gwine by.

Just then the vender broke forth in a most musical
voice :

Oh! Hannah, boil dat cabbage down,
  Hannah, boil 'em down,
And turn dem buckwheats round and round,
  Hannah, boil 'em down.
It's almost time to blow de horn,
  Hannah, boil 'em down,
To call de boys dat hoe de corn,
  Hannah, boil 'em down.

Hannah, boil 'em down,
    De cabbage just pulled out de ground,
  Boil 'em in de pot,
    And make him smoking hot.

.   .   .   .   .   .

Some like de cabbage made in krout,
  Hannah, boil 'em down,
Dey eat so much dey get de gout,
  Hannah, boil 'em down,
Dey chops 'em up and let dem spoil,
  Hannah, boil 'em down;
I'd rather hab my cabbage boiled,
  Hannah, boil 'em down.

Some say dat possum's in de pan,
  Hannah, boil 'em down,
Am de sweetest meat in all de land,
  Hannah, boil 'em down;
But dar is dat ole cabbage head,
  Hannah, boil 'em down,
I'll prize it, children, till I's dead,
  Hannah, boil 'em down.

This song, given in his inimitable manner, drew
the women to the windows, and the crowd around

the vegetable man in the street, and he soon disposed
of the contents of his cart. Other venders who
"toted" their commodities about in baskets on their
heads, took advantage of the musical man's company
to sell their own goods. A woman with some really
fine strawberries, put forth her claims in a very interesting song; the interest, however, centered more
upon the manner than the matter : —

> " I live fore miles out of town,
>   I am gwine to glory.
> My strawberries are sweet an' soun',
>   I am gwine to glory.
> I fotch 'em foré miles on my head,
>   I am gwine to glory.
> My chile is sick, an' husban' dead,
>   I am gwine to glory.
> Now's de time to get 'em cheap,
>   I am gwine to glory.
> Eat 'em wid yer bread an' meat,
>   I am gwine to glory.
> Come sinner get down on your knees,
>   I am gwine to glory.
> Eat dees strawberries when you please,
>   I am gwine to glory."

Upon the whole, the colored man of Virginia is a
very favorable physical specimen of his race; and
he has peculiarly fine, urbane manners. A stranger
judging from the surface of life here, would undoubt-
edly say that that they were a happy, well-to-do
people. Perhaps, also, he might say : "Ah, I see.
The negro is the same everywhere—a hewer of

wood, a peddler of vegetables, a wearer of the
waiter's white apron. Freedom has not altered his
status."

Such a judgment would be a very hasty one.
Nations are not educated in twenty years. There
are certain white men who naturally gravitate also
to these positions ; and we must remember that it is
only the present generation of negroes who have
been able to appropriate any share of the nobler
blessings of freedom. But the colored boys and
girls of Virginia are to-day vastly different from
what the colored boys and girls of fifteen or twenty
years ago were. The advancement and improvement is so great that it is not unreasonable to predict
from it a very satisfactory future.

The negro population here are greatly in the
majority, and formerly sent a member of their own
color to the State Senate, but through bribery and
ballot-box stuffing, a white Senator is now in Richmond. One negro here at a late election sold his
vote for a barrel of sugar. After he had voted and
taken his sugar home, he found it to be a barrel of
sand. I learn that his neighbors turned the laugh
upon him, and made him treat the whole company,
which cost him five dollars.

I would not have it supposed from what I have
said about the general condition of the blacks in
Virginia that there are none of a higher grade.
Far from it, for some of the best mechanics in the
State are colored men. In Richmond and Peters-
burg they have stores and carry on considerable

trade, both with the whites and their own race.
They are doing a great deal for education; many
send their sons and daughters North and West for
better advantages; and they are building some of
the finest churches in this State. The Second Baptist Church here pulled down a comparatively new
and fine structure, last year, to replace it with a
more splendid place of worship, simply because a
rival church of the same denomination had surpassed
them. I viewed the new edifice, and feel confident
it will compare favorably with any church on the
Back Bay, Boston.

The new building will seat three thousand persons,
and will cost, exclusive of the ground, one hundred
thousand dollars, all the brick and wood work of
which is being done by colored men.

CHAPTER XXIV.

THE education of the negro in the South is
the most important matter that we have to deal
with at present, and one that will claim precedence
of all other questions for many years to come.
When, soon after the breaking out of the Rebellion,
schools for the freedmen were agitated in the North,
and teachers dispatched from New England to go
down to teach the "poor contrabands," I went before
the proper authorities in Boston, and asked that a

place be given to one of our best-educated colored young ladies, who wanted to devote herself to the education of her injured race, and the offer was rejected, upon the ground that the "time for sending colored teachers had not come." This happened nearly twenty years ago. From that moment to the present, I have watched with painful interest the little progress made by colored men and women to become instructors of their own race in the Southern States.

Under the spur of the excitement occasioned by the Proclamation of Freedom, and the great need of schools for the blacks, thousands of dollars were contributed at the North, and agents sent to Great Britain, where generosity had no bounds. Money came in from all quarters, and some of the noblest white young women gave themselves up to the work of teaching the freedmen.

During the first three or four years, this field for teachers was filled entirely by others than members of the colored race, and yet it was managed by the "New England Freedmen's Association," made up in part by some of our best men and women.

But many energetic, educated colored young women and men, volunteered, and, at their own expense, went South and began private schools, and literally forced their way into the work. This was followed by a few appointments, which in every case proved that colored teachers for colored people was the great thing needed. Upon the foundations laid by these small schools, some of the most splendid educational institutions in the South have sprung up. Fisk, Howard, Atlanta, Hampton, Tennessee Central, Virginia Central, and Straight, are some of the most prominent. These are all under the control and management of the whites, and are accordingly conducted upon the principle of whites for teachers and blacks for pupils. And yet each of the above institutions are indebted to the sympathy felt for the negro, for their very existence. Some of these colleges give more encouragement to the negro to become an instructor, than others; but, none however, have risen high enough to measure the black man independent of his color.

At Petersburg I found a large, fine building for public schools for colored youth; the principal, a white man, with six assistants, but not one colored teacher amongst them. Yet Petersburg has turned out some most excellent colored teachers, two of whom I met at Suffolk, with small schools. These young ladies had graduated with honors at one of our best institutions, and yet could not obtain a position as teacher in a public school, where the pupils were only their own race.

At Nashville, the School Board was still more unjust, for they employed teachers who would not allow their colored scholars to recognize them on the streets, and for doing which, the children were reprimanded, and the action of the teachers approved by the Board of Education.

It is generally known that all the white teachers in our colored public schools feel themselves above their work; and the fewest number have any communication whatever with their pupils outside the school-room. Upon receiving their appointments and taking charge of their schools some of them have been known to announce to their pupils that under no circumstances were they to recognize or speak to them on the streets. It is very evident that these people have no heart in the work they are doing, and simply from day to day go through the mechanical form of teaching our children for the pittance they receive as a salary. While teachers who have no interest in the children they instruct, except for the salary they get, are employed in the public schools and in the Freedman's Colleges, hundreds of colored men and women, who are able to stand the most rigid examination, are idle, or occupying places far beneath what they deserve.

It is to be expected that the public schools will, to a greater or less extent, be governed by the political predilections of the parties in power; but we ought to look for better things from Fisk, Hampton, Howard, Atlanta, Tennessee Central and Virginia Central, whose walls sprung up by money raised from appeals made for negro education.

There are, however, other educational institutions of which I have not made mention, and which deserve the patronage of the benevolent everywhere. These are: Wilberforce, Berea, Payne Institute, in South Carolina, Waco College, in Texas, and Storer College, at Harper's Ferry.

Wilberforce is well known, and is doing a grand

work. It has turned out some of the best of our
scholars, — men whose labors for the elevation of
their race cannot be too highly commended.

Storer College, at Harper's Ferry, looks down
upon the ruins of "John Brown's Fort." In the
ages to come, Harper's Ferry will be sought out by
the traveller from other lands. Here at the conflu-
ence of the Potomac and the Shenandoah Rivers, on
a point just opposite the gap through which the
united streams pass the Blue Ridge, on their course
toward the ocean, stands the romantic town, and a little
above it, on a beautiful eminence, is Storer, an institution, and of whose officers I cannot speak too highly.

I witnessed, with intense interest, the earnest
efforts of these good men and women, in their glori-
ous work of the elevation of my race. And while
the benevolent of the North are giving of their
abundance, I would earnestly beg them not to forget
Storer College, at Harper's Ferry.

The other two, of which I have made mention,
are less known, but their students are numerous and
well trained. *Both these schools are in the South,*
and both are owned and managed by colored men,
free from the supposed necessity of having white
men to do their *thinking,* and therein ought to
receive the special countenance of all who believe in
giving the colored people a chance to paddle their
own canoe.

I failed, however, to find schools for another part
of our people, which appear to be much needed.
For many years in the olden time the South was

noted for its beautiful Quadroon women. Bottles of
ink, and reams of paper, have been used to portray
the "finely-cut and well-moulded features," the
"silken curls," the "dark and brilliant eyes," the
"splendid forms," the "fascinating smiles," and "accomplished manners" of these impassioned and vol-
uptuous daughters of the two races,—the unlawful
product of the crime of human bondage. When we
take into consideration the fact that no safeguard was
ever thrown around virtue, and no inducement held
out to slave-women to be pure and chaste, we will
not be surprised when told that immorality pervaded
the domestic circle in the cities and towns of the
South to an extent unknown in the Northern States.
Many a planter's wife has dragged out a miserable
existence, with an aching heart, at seeing her place
in the husband's affections usurped by the unadorned
beauty and captivating smiles of her waiting-maid.
Indeed, the greater portion of the colored women,
in the days of slavery, had no greater aspiration
than that of becoming the finely-dressed mistress of
some white man. Although freedom has brought
about a new order of things, and our colored women
are making rapid strides to rise above the dark
scenes of the past, yet the want of protection to our
people since the old-time whites have regained power,
places a large number of the colored young women
of the cities and towns at the mercy of bad colored
men, or worse white men. To save these from des-
truction, institutions ought to be established in every
large city.

Mrs. Julia G. Thomas, a very worthy lady, deeply interested in the welfare of her sex, has a small institution for orphans and friendless girls, where they will have a home, schooling, and business training, to fit them to enter life with a prospect of success. Mrs. Thomas' address is 190 High Street, Nashville, Tennessee.

CHAPTER XXV.

AMONG the causes of that dissatisfaction of the colored people in the South which has produced the exodus therefrom, there is one that lies beneath the surface and is concealed from even an astute observer, if he is a stranger to that section. This cause consists in certain legislative enactments that have been passed in most of the cotton States, ostensibly for other purposes, but really for the purpose of establishing in those States a system of peonage similar to, if not worse than, that which prevails in Mexico. This is the object of a statute passed by the Legislature of Mississippi, in March, 1878. The title of the act, whether intentionally so or not, is certainly misleading. It is entitled "An act to reduce the judiciary expenses of the State." But how it can possibly have that effect is beyond human wisdom to perceive. It, however, does operate, and is used in such a way as to enslave a large number of negroes, who have not even been convicted of the slightest offence against the laws.

The act provides that "all persons convicted and committed to the jail of the county, except those committed to jail for contempt of court, and except those sentenced to imprisonment in the Penitentiary, shall be delivered to a contractor, to be by him kept and worked under the provisions of this act; and all persons committed to jail, except those not entitled to bail, may also, with their consent, be committed to said contractor and worked under this act before conviction." But Sect. 5, of the act provides ample and cogent machinery to produce the necessary consent on the part of the not yet convicted prisoner to work for the contractor. In that section it is provided "that if any person committed to jail for an offence that is bailable shall not consent to be committed to the safe keeping and custody of said contractor, and to work for said contractor, and to work for the same under this act, the prisoner shall be entitled to receive only six ounces of bacon, or ten ounces of beef, and one pound of bread and water."

This section also provides that any prisoner not consenting to work before his conviction for the contractor, and that too, without compensation, "If said prisoner shall afterward be convicted, he shall, nevertheless, work under said contractor a sufficient term to pay all cost of prosecution, including the regular jail fees for keeping and feeding him. The charge for feeding him, upon the meagre bill of fare above stated, is twenty cents a day. Now, it cannot be denied that the use made of this law

is to deprive the negro of his natural right to
choose his own employer; and in the following
manner: Let us suppose a case, and such cases
are constantly occurring. A is a cotton planter,
owns three or four thousand acres of land, and has
forty, fifty, or one hundred negro families on his
plantation. At the expiration of the year, a negro
proposes to leave the plantation of A, and try to
better his condition by making a more advantageous
bargain with B, or C, for another year. If A can
prevent the negro from leaving him in no other way,
this statute puts full power in his hands. A trumps
up some petty charge against the negro, threatens
to have him arrested and committed to jail. The
negro knows how little it will take to commit him to
jail, and that then he must half starve on a pound of
bread and water and six ounces of bacon a day, or
work for the contractor for nothing until he can
be tried; and when tried he must run the risk of
conviction, which is not slight, though he may be
ever so innocent. Avarice — unscrupulous avarice
—is pursuing him, and with little power to resist,
there being no healthy public sentiment in favor of
fair play to encourage him, he yields, and becomes
the peon of his oppressor.

I found the whipping-post in full operation in
Virginia, and heard of its being enforced in other
States. I inquired of a black man what he thought
of the revival of that mode of punishment. He replied, "Well, sar, I don't ker for it, kase dey treats
us all alike; dey whips whites at de poss jess as dey

do de blacks, an' dat's what I calls equality before de law."

A friend of mine meeting a man who was leaving Arkansas, on account of the revival of her old slave laws, the following conversation occurred, showing that the oppression of the blacks extends to all the States South.

"You come from Arkansas, I understand?"

"Yes."

"What wages do you generally get for your work?"

"Since about '68, we've been getting about two bits a day — that's twenty cents. Then there are some people that work by the month, and at the end of the month they are either put off or cheated out of their money entirely. Property and goods are worth nothing to a black man there. He can't get his price for them; he gets just what the white man chooses to give him. Some people who raise from ten to fifteen bales of cotton sometimes have hardly enough to cover their body and feet. This goes on while the white man gets the price he asks for his goods. This is unfair, and as long as we pay taxes we want justice, right, and equality before the people."

"What taxes do you pay?"

"A man that owns a house and lot has to pay about twenty-six dollars a year; and if he has a mule worth about one hundred and fifty dollars they tax him two dollars and a half extra. If they see you have money—say you made three thousand dollars — you'd soon see some bill about taxes, land lease and the other coming in for about two thousand of it. They charge a black man thirteen dollars where they would only charge a white man one or two. Now, there's a man," pointing to a portly old fellow, "who had to run away from his house, farm, and all. It is for this we leave Arkansas. We want freedom, and I say, 'Give me liberty or give me death.' We took up arms and fought for our country, so we ought to have our rights."

"How about the schooling you receive?"

"We can't vote, still we have to pay taxes to support schools for the others. I got my education in New Orleans and paid for it, too. I have six children, and though I pay taxes not one of them has any schooling from the public schools. The taxes and rent are so heavy that the children have to work when they are as young as ten years. That's the way it is down there."

"Did you have any teachers from the North?"

"There were some teachers from the North who came down there, but they were run out. They were paid so badly and treated so mean that they had to go."

" What county did you live in?"

" Phillips County."

" How many schools were in that county?"

" About five."

" When do they open?"

" About once every two years and keep open for two or three weeks. And then they have a certain

kind of book for the children. Those that have
dogs, cats, hogs, cows, horses, and all sorts of ani-
mals in them. They keep the children in these and
never let them get out of them."

"Have you any colleges in the State for colored
men?"

"No, they haven't got any colleges and don't allow
any. The other day I asked a Republican how was
it that so many thousands of dollars were taken for
colleges and we didn't get any good of it? He said,
'The bill didn't pass, somehow.' And now I guess
those fellows spent all that money."

"As a general thing, then, the people are very
ignorant?"

"Yes, sir; the colored man that's got education is
like some people that's got religion — he hides it
under a bushel; if he didn't, and stood up for his
rights as a citizen, he would soon become the game
of some of the Ku-Klux clubs."

Having succeeded in getting possession of power
in the South, and driving the black voters from the
polls at elections, and also having them counted in
National Representation, the ex-rebels will soon have
a power which they never before enjoyed. Had
the slaveholders in 1860 possessed the right of rep-
resenting their slaves fully instead of partly in Con-
gress and in the Electoral College, they would have
ruled this country indefinitely in the interest of
slavery. It was supposed that by the result of the
war, freedom profited and the slaveholding class lost
power forever. But the very act which conferred

the full right of representation upon the three million freedmen, by the help of the policy, has placed an instrument in the hands of the rebel conspirators which they will use to pervert and defeat the objects of the Constitutional amendments. Through this policy the thirty-five additional electoral votes given to the freedmen have been "turned over to the Democratic party." Aye, more than that; they have been turned over to the ex-rebels, who will use them in the cause of oppression scarcely second in hatefulness to that of chattel slavery. In a contest with the solid South, therefore, the party of freedom and justice will have greater odds to overcome than it did in 1860, and the Southern oligarchs hold a position which is well nigh impregnable for whatever purpose they choose to use it.

Of the large number of massacres perpetrated upon the blacks in the South, since the ex-rebels have come into power, I give one instance, which will show the inhumanity of the whites. This outrage occurred in Gibson County, Tennessee. The report was first circulated that the blacks in great numbers were armed, and were going to commit murder upon the whites. This created the excitement that it was intended to, and the whites in large bodies, armed to the teeth, went through Gibson, and adjoining counties, disarming the blacks, taking from them their only means of defence, and arresting all objectionable blacks that they could find, taking them to Trenton and putting them in jail.

The following account of the wanton massacre, is from the *Memphis Appeal:* —

"About four hundred armed, disguised, mounted men entered this town at two o'clock this morning, proceeded to the jail, and demanded the keys of the jailor, Mr. Alexander. He refused to give up the keys. Sheriff Williams, hearing the noise, awoke and went to the jail, and refused to surrender the keys to the maskers, telling them that he did not have the keys. They cocked their pistols, and he refused again to give them the keys, whereupon the Captain of the company ordered the masked men to draw their pistols and cock them, swearing they would have the keys or shoot the jailor. The jailor dared them to shoot, and said they were too cowardly to shoot. They failed to do this. Then they threatened to tear down the jail or get the prisoners. The jailor told them that rather than they should tear down the jail he would give them the keys if they would go with him to his office. The jailor did this because he saw that the men were determined to break through. 'They were all disguised. Then they came,' says the Sheriff, 'and got the keys from my office, and giving three or four yells, went to the jail, unlocked it, took out the sixteen negroes who had been brought here from Pickettsville (Gibson), and, tying their hands, escorted them away. They proceeded on the Huntingdon road without saying a word, and in fifteen minutes I heard shots. In company with several citizens I proceeded down the road in the direction taken by the men and prison-

ers, and just beyond the river bridge, half a mile
from town, I found four negroes dead, on the
ground, their bodies riddled with bullets, and two
wounded. We saw no masked men. Ten negroes
yet remain unaccounted for. Leaving the dead
bodies where we found them, we brought the two
wounded negroes to town, and summoned medical
aid. Justice J. M. Caldwell held an inquest on the
bodies, the verdict being in accordance with the facts
that death resulted from shots inflicted by guns in
the hands of unknown parties. The inquest was
held about eight o'clock this morning. These are
all the facts relative to the shooting I can give you.
I did my duty to prevent the rescue of the negroes,
but found it useless to oppose the men, one of whom
said there were four hundred in the band.'

"Night before last the guard that brought the
prisoners from Pickettsville remained. No fears or
intimations of the attempted rescue were then heard
of or feared. This morning, learning that four or
five hundred armed negroes, on the Jackson road,
were marching into town to burn the buildings and
kill the people, the citizens immediately organized,
armed, and prepared for active defence, and went
out to meet the negroes, scouted the whole country
around but found no armed negroes. The citizens
throughout the country commenced coming into town
by hundreds. Men came from Union City, Kenton,
Troy, Rutherford, Dyer Station, Skull Bone, and
the whole country, but found no need of their services. The two wounded negroes will die. The

bodies of the ten other negroes taken from the jail were found in the river bottom about a mile from town.

" We blush for our State, and with the shame of the bloody murder, the disgraceful defiance of law, of order, and of decency full upon us, are at a loss for language with which to characterize a deed that, if the work of Comanches or Modocs, would arouse every man in the Union for a speedy vengeance on the perpetrators. To-day, we must hold up to merited reprobation and condemnation the armed men who besieged the Trenton Jail, and wantonly as wickedly, without anything like justification, took thence the unarmed negroes there awaiting trial by the courts, and brutally shot them to death; and, too, with a show of barbarity altogether as unnecessary as the massacre was unjustifiable. To say that we are not, in any county in the State, strong enough to enforce the law, is to pronounce a libel upon the whole Commonwealth. We are as a thousand to one in moral and physical force to the negro; we are in possession of the State, of all the machinery of Government, and at a time more momentous than any we ever hope to see again have proved our capacity to sustain the law's executive officers and maintain the laws. Why, then, should we now, in time of profound peace, subvert the law and defy its administrators? Why should we put the Government of our own selection under our feet, and defy and set at naught the men whom we have elected to enforce the laws, and this ruthlessly and savagely, without any of the forms, even, that usually attend on the administration of the wild behests of Judge Lynch? And all without color of extenuation; for no sane man who has regard for the truth will pretend to say that because the unfortunate negroes were arrested as the ringleaders of a threatening and armed band that had fired upon two white men, they were, therefore, worthy of death, and without the forms of law, in a State controlled and governed by law-abiding men."

No one was ever punished, or even an attempt made to ferret out the perpetrators of this foul murder. And the infliction of the death punishment, by "Lynch Law," on colored persons for the slightest offence, proves that there is really no abatement in this hideous race prejudice that prevails throughout the South.

CHAPTER XXVI.

YEARS ago, when the natural capabilities of the races were more under discussion than now, the negro was always made to appear to greater disadvantage than the rest of mankind. The public mind is not yet free from this false theory, nor has the colored man done much of late years to change this opinion. Long years of training of any people to a particular calling, seems to fit them for that vocation more than for any other. Thus, the Jews, inured to centuries of money-lending and pawn-broking, they, as a race, stick to it as if they were created for that business alone.

The training of the Arabs for long excursions through wild deserts, makes them the master roam-ers of the world. The Gypsies, brought up to camping out and trading in horses, send forth the idea that they were born for it. The black man's position as a servant, for many generations, has not only made the other races believe that is his legiti-mate sphere, but he himself feels more at home in a white apron and a towel on his arm, than with a quill behind his ear and a ledger before him.

That a colored man takes to the dining-room and the kitchen, as a duck does to water, only proves that like other races, his education has entered into his blood. This is not theory, this is not poetry; but stern truth. Our people prefer to be servants.

This may be to some extent owing to the fact that the organ of alimentativeness is more prominently formed in the negro's make-up, than in that of almost any other people.

During several trips in the cars between Nashville and Columbia, I noticed that the boy who sold news-papers and supplied the passengers with fruit, had a basket filled with candy and cakes. The first time I was on his car he offered me the cakes, which I declined, but bought a paper. Watching him I ob-served that when colored persons entered the car, he would offer them the cakes which they seldom failed

to purchase. One day as I took from him a newspaper, I inquired of him why he always offered
cakes to the colored passengers. His reply was : —
"Oh ! they always buy something to eat."

"Do they purchase more cakes than white people ? "

"Yes," was the response.

"Why do they buy your cakes and candy ? " I
asked.

"Well, sir, the colored people seem always to be
hungry. Never see anything like it. They don't
buy papers, but they are always eating."

Just then we stopped at Franklin, and three colored passengers came in. "Now," continued the
cake boy, "you'll see how they'll take the cakes,"
and he started for them, but had to pass their seats
to shut the door that had been left open. In going
by, one of the men, impatient to get a cake, called,
"Here, here, come here wid yer cakes."

The peddler looked at me and laughed. He sold
each one a cake, and yet it was not ten o'clock in
the morning.

Not long since, in Massachusetts, I succeeded in
getting a young man pardoned from our State prison,
where he had been confined for more than ten years,
and where he had learned a good trade.

I had already secured him a situation where he
was to receive three dollars per day to commence
with, with a prospect of an advance of wages.

As we were going to his boarding place, and after
I had spent some time in advising him to turn over
a new leaf and to try and elevate himself, we passed

one of our best hotels. My ward at once stopped, began snuffing as if he "smelt a mice." I looked at him, watched his countenance as it lighted up and his eyes sparkled; I inquired what was the matter. With a radiant smile he replied, "I smell good wittles; what place is that?"

"It is the Revere House," I said.

"Wonder if I could get a place to wait on table there?" he asked.

I thought it a sorry comment on my efforts to instil into him some self-respect. This young man had learned the shoemaking trade, and at a McKay machine, I understood that he could earn from three dollars and a half to five dollars per day.

A dozen years ago, two colored young men commenced the manufacture of one of the necessary commodities of the day. After running the establishment some six or eight months successfully, they sold out to white men, who now employ more than one hundred hands. Both of the colored men are at their legitimate callings; one is a waiter in a private house, the other is a porter on a sleeping car.

The failure of these young men to carry on a manufacturing business was mainly owing to a want of training, in a business point of view. No man is fit for a profession or a trade, unless he has learned it.

Extravagance in dress is a great and growing evil with our people. I am acquainted with a lady in Boston who wears a silk dress costing one hundred and thirty dollars. She lives in two rooms, and her husband is a hair-dresser.

Since the close of the war, a large number of freedmen settled in Massachusetts, where they became servants, the most of them. These people surpass in dress, the wealthiest merchants of the city.

A young man, now a servant in a private house, sports a sixty-dollar overcoat while he works for twenty dollars per month.

A woman who cooks for five dollars per week, in Arlington Street, swings along every Sunday in a hundred-dollar silk dress, and a thirty-dollar hat. She cannot read or write.

Go to our churches on the Sabbath, and see the silk, the satin, the velvet, and the costly feathers, and talk with the uneducated wearers, and you will see at once the main hindrance to self-elevation.

To elevate ourselves and our children, we must cultivate self-denial. Repress our appetites for luxuries and be content with clothing ourselves in garments becoming our means and our incomes. The adaptation and the deep inculcation of the principles of total abstinence from all intoxicants. The latter is a pre-requisite for success in all the relations of life.

Emerging from the influence of oppression, taught from early experience to have no confidence in the whites, we have little or none in our own race, or even in ourselves.

We need more self-reliance, more confidence in the ability of our own people; more manly inde-

pendence, a higher standard of moral, social, and
literary culture.   Indeed, we need a union of effort
to remove the dark shadow of ignorance that now
covers the land.   While the barriers of prejudice
keep us morally and socially from educated white
society, we must make a strong effort to raise ourselves from the common level where emancipation
and the new order of things found us.

We possess the elements of successful development; but we need live men and women to make
this development.   The last great struggle for our
rights; the battle for our own civilization, is entirely
with ourselves, and the problem is to be solved by
us.

We must use our spare time, day and night, to
educate ourselves.   Let us have night schools for
the adults, and not be ashamed to attend them.   Encourage our own literary men and women; subscribe
for, and be sure and pay for papers published by
colored men.   Don't stop to inquire if the paper
will live; but encourage it, and make it live.

With the exception of a few benevolent societies,
we are separated as far from each other as the east is
from the west.

CHAPTER XXVII.

UNION is strength, has long since passed into
a proverb.   The colored people of the South
should at once form associations, combine and make

them strong, and live up to them by all hazards.
All civilized races have risen by means of combination and co-operation. The Irishman, the German,
the Frenchman, all come to this country poor, and
they stay here but a short time before you see them
succeeding in some branch of business.   This
success is not the result of individual effort — it is
the result of combination and co-operation. Whatever an Irishman has to spend he puts in the till of
one of his own countrymen, and that accounts for
Irish success.

A German succeeds in this country because all his
fellow-countrymen patronize him in whatever business he engages. A German will put himself to
inconvenience, and go miles out of his way to spend
money with one of his own race and nationality.

With all his fickleness, the Frenchman never for-
gets to find out and patronize one of his own people.
Italians flock together and stand by each other, right
or wrong. The Chinese are clannish, and stick by
one another. The Caucasian race is the foremost
in the world in everything that pertains to advanced
civilization, — simply owing to the fact that an Eng-
glishman never passes the door of a countryman to
patronize another race ; and a Yankee is a Yankee
all the days of his life, and will never desert his
colors. But where is the Negro?

A gentlemanly and well-informed colored man
came to me a few days since, wishing to impart to
me some important information, and he commenced
by saying : "Now, Doctor, what I am going to tell

you, you may rely on its being true, because I got
it from a white man — no nigger told me this."

On Duke Street, in Alexandria, Va., resides an
Irishman, who began business in that place a dozen
years ago, with two jugs, one filled with whiskey,
the other with molasses, a little pork, some vegetables, sugar and salt. On the opposite side of the
street was our good friend, Mr. A. S. Perpener.
The latter had a respectable provision store, minus
the whiskey. Colored people inhabited the greater
part of the street. Did they patronize their own
countryman? Not a bit of it. The Irishman's
business increased rapidly; he soon enlarged his
premises, adding wood and coal to his salables.
Perpener did the same, but the blacks passed by and
went over on the other side, gave their patronage to
the son of Erin, who now has houses "to let," but
he will not rent them to colored tenants.

The Jews, though scattered throughout the world,
are still Jews. Their race and their religion they
have maintained in all countries and all ages. They
never forsake each other. If they fall out, over
some trade, they make up in time to combine against
the rest of mankind. Shylock says: "I will buy
with you, sell with you, talk with you, walk with
you, and so following; but I will not eat with you,
drink with you, nor pray with you." Thus, the
Jew, with all his love of money, will not throw off
his religion to satisfy others, and for this we honor
him.

It is the misfortune of our race that the impres-

sion prevails that "one nigger is as good as another."
Now this is a great error; there are colored men in
this country as far ahead of others of their own race
as Webster and Sumner were superior to the average
white man.

Then, again, we have no confidence in each
other. We consider the goods from the store of a
white man necessarily better than can be purchased
from a colored man.

No man ever succeeded who lacked confidence in
himself. No race ever did or ever will prosper or
make a respectable history which has no confidence
in its own nationality.

Those who do not appreciate their own people
will not be appreciated by other people. If a white
man will pat a colored man on the shoulder, bow to
him, and call him "Mr.," he will go a mile out of his
way to patronize him, if in doing so he passes a
first-class dealer of his own race. I asked a colored
man in Columbia if he patronized Mr. Frierson.
He said, "No." I inquired, "Why?" "He never
invited me to his house in his life," was the reply.

"Does the white man you deal with invite you?"

"No."

"Then, why do you expect Mr. Frierson to
do it?"

"Oh! he's a nigger and I look for more from him
than I do from a white man." So it is clear that
this is the result of jealousy.

The recent case of the ill-treatment of Cadet
Whittaker, at West Point, shows most clearly the

unsuspecting character of the negro, when dealing with whites. Although Whittaker had been repeatedly warned that an attack was to be made upon him, and especially told to look out for the assault the very night that the crime was committed, he laid down with his room-door unfastened, went off into a sound sleep, with no weapon or means of defence near him. This was, for all the world, like a negro. A Yankee would have had a revolver with every chamber loaded; an Irishman would have slept with one eye open, and a stout shillalah in his right hand, and in all probability somebody would have had a nice funeral after the attack. But that want of courage and energy, so characteristic of the race, permitted one of the foulest crimes to be perpetrated which has come to light for years.

But the most disgraceful part in this whole transaction lies with the Court of Investigation, now being conducted at West Point under the supervision of United States officials. The unfeeling and unruly cadets that outraged Whittaker, no doubt, laid a deep plan to cover up their tracks, and this was to make it appear that their victim had inflicted upon himself his own injuries. And acting upon this theory, one of the young scamps, who had no doubt been rehearsing for the occasion, volunteered to show the Court how the negro could have practised the imposition.

And, strange to say, these sage *investigators* sat quietly and looked on while the young ruffian laid down upon the floor, tied himself, and explained how the thing was done.

If the victim had been a white man and his persecutors black, does any one believe for a moment that such a theory would have been listened to?

Generations of oppression have done their work too thoroughly to have its traces wiped away in a dozen years. The race must be educated out of the ignorance in which it at present dwells, and lifted to a level with other races. Colored lawyers, doctors, artisans and mechanics, starve for patronage, while the negro is begging the white man to do his work. Combinations have made other races what they are to-day.

The great achievements of scientific men could not have been made practical by individual effort. The great works of genius could never have benefited the world, had those who composed them been mean and selfish. All great and useful enterprises have succeeded through the influence and energy of numbers.

I would not have it thought that all colored men are to be bought by the white man's smiles, or to be frightened by intimidation. Far from it. In all the Southern States we have some of the noblest specimens of mankind,—men of genius, refinement, courage and liberality, ready to do and to die for the race.

CHAPTER XXVIII.

ADVICE upon the formation of Literary Associations, and total abstinence from all intoxications is needed, and I will give it to you in this chapter. The time for colored men and women to organize for self-improvement has arrived. Moral, social, and intellectual development, should be the main attainment of the negro race. Colored people have so long been in the habit of aping the whites, and often not the better class either, that I fear this characteristic in them, more than anything else. A large percentage of them being waiters, they see a great deal of drinking in white society of the "Upper Ten." Don't follow their bad example. Take warning by their degradation.

During the year 1879, Boston sent four hundred drunken women to the Sherborn prison; while two private asylums are full, many of them from Boston's first families. Therefore, I beseech you to never allow the intoxicant to enter your circles.

It is bad enough for men to lapse into habits of drunkenness. A drunken husband, a drunken father — only those patient, heart-broken, shame-faced wives and children on whom this great cross of suffering is laid, can estimate the misery which it brings.

But a drunken girl — a drunken wife — a drunken mother — is there for woman a deeper depth? Home made hideous — children disgraced, neglected, and maltreated.

Remember that all this comes from the first glass. The wine may be pleasant to the taste, and may for the time being, furnish happiness; but it must never be forgotten that whatever degree of exhiliration may be produced in a healthy person by the use of wine, it will most certainly be succeeded by a degree of nervous depression proportioned to the amount of previous excitement.   Hence the immoderate use of wine, or its habitual indulgence, debilitates the brain and nervous system, paralyzes the intellectual powers, impairs the functions of the stomach, produces a perverted appetite for a renewal of the dele- terious beverage, or a morbid imagination, which destroys man's usefulness.

The next important need with our people, is the cultivation of habits of business.   We have been so long a dependent race, so long looking to the white as our leaders, and being content with doing the drudgery of life, that most who commence busi- ness for themselves are likely to fail, because of want of a knowledge of what we undertake.   As the education of a large percentage of the colored people is of a fragmentary character, having been gained by little and little here and there, and must necessarily be limited to a certain degree, we should use our spare hours in study and form associations for moral, social, and literary culture.   We must aim to enlighten ourselves and to influence others to higher associations.

Our work lies primarily with the inward culture, at the springs and sources of individual life and character, seeking everywhere to encourage, and assist to the fullest emancipation of the human mind from ignorance, inviting the largest liberty of thought, and the utmost possible exaltation of life into approximation to the loftier standard of culti-

vated character. Feeling that the literature of our
age is the reflection of the existing manners and
modes of thought, etherealized and refined in the
alembic of genius, we should give our principal encouragement to literature, bringing before our associations the importance of original essays, selected
readings, and the cultivation of the musical talent.

If we need any proof of the good that would
accrue from such cultivation, we have only to look
back and see the wonderful influence of Homer over
the Greeks, of Virgil and Horace over the Romans,
of Dante and Ariosto over the Italians, of Goethe
and Schiller over the Germans, of Racine and Vol-
taire over the French, of Shakespeare and Milton
over the English. The imaginative powers of these
men, wrought into verse or prose, have been the
theme of the king in his palace, the lover in his
dreamy moods, the farmer in the harvest field,
the mechanic in the work-shop, the sailor on the
high seas, and the prisoner in his gloomy cell.

Indeed, authors possess the most gifted and fertile
minds who combine all the graces of style with
rare, fascinating powers of language, eloquence,
wit, humor, pathos, genius and learning. And to
draw knowledge from such sources should be one
of the highest aims of man. The better elements of
society can only be brought together by organizing
societies and clubs.

The cultivation of the mind is the superstructure
of the moral, social and religious character, which
will follow us into our every-day life, and make us

what God intended us to be — the noblest instruments of His creative power. Our efforts should be to imbue our minds with broader and better views of science, literature, and a nobleness of spirit that ignores petty aims of patriotism, glory, or. mere personal aggrandizement. It is said, never a shadow falls that does not leave a permanent impress of its image, a monument of its passing presence. Every character is modified by association. Words, the image of the ideas, are more impressive than shadows; actions, embodied thoughts, more enduring than aught material. Believing these truths, then, I say, for every thought expressed, ennobling in its tendency and elevating to Christian dignity and manly honor, God will reward us. Permanent success depends upon intrinsic worth. The best way to have a public character is to have a private one.

The great struggle for our elevation is now with ourselves. We may talk of Hannibal, Euclid, Phyllis, Wheatly, Benjamin Bannaker, and Toussaint L'Overture, but the world will ask us for our men and women of the day. We cannot live upon the past; we must hew out a reputation that will stand the test, one that we have a legitimate right to. To do this, we must imitate the best examples set us by the cultivated whites, and by so doing we will teach them that they can claim no superiority on account of race.

The efforts made by oppressed nations or communities to throw off their chains, entitles them to, and gains for them the respect of mankind. This, the

blacks never made, or what they did, was so feeble
as scarcely to call for comment. The planning of
Denmark Vesey for an insurrection in South Carolina, was noble, and deserved a better fate; but he
was betrayed by the race that he was attempting to
serve.

Nat Turner's strike for liberty was the outburst of
feelings of an insane man, — made so by slavery.
True, the negro did good service at the battles of
Wagner, Honey Hill, Port Hudson, Millikin's Bend,
Poison Springs, Olustee and Petersburg. Yet it
would have been far better if they had commenced
earlier, or had been under leaders of their own
color. The St. Domingo revolution brought forth
men of courage. But the subsequent course of the
people as a government, reflects little or no honor
on the race. They have floated about like a ship
without a rudder, ever since the expulsion of
Rochambeau.

The fact is the world likes to see the exhibition of
pluck on the part of an oppressed people, even
though they fail in their object. It is these outbursts of the love of liberty that gains respect and
sympathy for the enslaved. Therefore, I bid God
speed to the men and women of the South, in their
effort to break the long spell of lethargy that hangs
over the race. Don't be too rash in starting, but
prepare to go, and "don't stand upon the order of
going, but go." By common right, the South is the
negro's home. Born, and "raised" there, he cleared
up the lands, built the cities, fed and clothed the

whites, nursed their children, earned the money to educate their sons and daughters; by the negro's labor churches were built and clergymen paid.

For two hundred years the Southern whites lived a lazy life at the expense of the negro's liberty. When the rebellion came, the blacks, trusted and true to the last, protected the families and homes of white men while they were away fighting the Government. The South is the black man's home; yet if he cannot be protected in his rights he should leave. Where white men of liberal views can get no protection, the colored man must not look for it. Follow the example of other oppressed races, strike out for new territory If suffering is the result, let it come; others have suffered before you. Look at the Irish, Germans, French, Italians, and other races, who have come to this country, gone to the West, and are now enjoying the blessings of liberty and plenty; while the negro is discussing the question of whether he should leave the South or not, simply because he was born there.

While they are thus debating the subject, their old oppressors, seeing that the negro has touched the right chord, forbid his leaving the country. Georgia has made it a penal offence to invite the blacks to emigrate, and one negro is already in prison for wishing to better the condition of his fellows. This is the same spirit that induced the people of that State to offer a reward of five thousand dollars, in 1835, for the head of Garrison. No people has borne oppression like the negro, and no race has been so much imposed upon. Go to his own land. Ask the Dutch boor whence comes his contempt and inward dislike to the negro, the Hottentot, and Caffre; ask him for his warrant to reduce these unhappy races to slavery; he will point to the fire-arms suspended over the mantle-piece — "There is my right."

Want of independence is the colored man's greatest fault. In the present condition of the Southern States, with the lands in the hands of a shoddy, ignorant, superstitious, rebellious, and negro-hating population, the blacks cannot be independent. Then emigrate to get away from the surroundings that keep you down where you are. All cannot go, even if it were desirable; but those who remain will have a better opportunity. The planters will then have to pursue a different policy. The right of the negroes to make the best terms they can, will have to be recognized, and what was before presumption that called for repression will now be tolerated as among the privileges of freedom. The ability of the negroes to change their location will also turn public sentiment against bull-dozing.

Two hundred years have demonstrated the fact that the negro is the manual laborer of that section, and without him agriculture will be at a stand-still.

The negro will for pay perform any service under heaven, no matter how repulsive or full of hardship, He will sing his old plantation melodies and walk about the cotton fields in July and August, when the toughest white man seeks an awning. Heat is his element. He fears no malaria in the rice swamps, where a white man's life is not worth sixpence.

Then, I say, leave the South and starve the whites into a realization of justice and common sense. Remember that tyrants never relinquish their grasp upon their victims until they are forced to.

Whether the blacks emigrate or not, I say to them, keep away from the cities and towns. Go into the country. Go to work on farms.

If you stop in the city, get a profession or a trade, but keep in mind that a good trade is better than a poor profession.

In Boston there are a large number of colored professionals, especially in the law, and a majority of whom are better fitted for farm service, mechanical branches, or for driving an ash cart.

Persons should not select professions for the name of being a "professional," nor because they think they will lead an easy life. An honorable, lucrative and faithfully-earned professional reputation, is a career of honesty, patience, sobriety, toil and Christian zeal.

No drone can fill such a position. Select the profession or trade that your education, inclination, strength of mind and body will support, and then give your time to the work that you have undertaken, and work, work.

Once more I say to those who cannot get remunerative employment at the South, emigrate.

Some say, "stay and fight it out, contend for your rights, don't let the old rebels drive you away, the

country is as much yours as theirs." That kind of
talk will do very well for men who have comfortable
homes out of the South, and law to protect them;
but for the negro, with no home, no food, no work,
the land-owner offering him conditions whereby he
can do but little better than starve, such talk is non-
sense. Fight out what? Hunger? Poverty? Cold?
Starvation? Black men, emigrate.

CHAPTER XXIX.

IN America, the negro stands alone as a race. He
is without mate or fellow in the great family of
man. Whatever progress he makes, it must be
mainly by his own efforts. This is an unfortunate
fact, and for which there seems to be no remedy.

All history demonstrates the truth that amalgamation is the great civilizer of the races of men.
Wherever a race, clan, or community have kept
themselves together, prohibiting by law, usage, or
common consent, inter-marriage with others, they
have made little or no progress. The Jews, a dis-
tinct and isolated people, are good only at driving a
bargain and getting rich. The Gipsies commence
and stop with trading horses. The Irish, in their
own country, are dull. The Coptic race form but a
handful of what they were—those builders, un-
equalled in ancient or modern times. What has
become of them? Where are the Romans? What

races have they destroyed? What races have they
supplanted? For fourteen centuries they lorded it
over the semi-civilized world; and now they are of
no more note than the ancient Scythians, or Mongols,
Copts, or Tartars. An un-amalgamated, inactive
people will decline. Thus it was with the Mexicans,
when Cortes marched on Mexico, and the Peruvians,
when Pizarro marched on Peru.

The Britons were a dull, lethargic people before
their country was invaded, and the hot, romantic
blood of Julius Cæsar and William of Normandy
coursed through their veins.

Caractacus, king of the Britons, was captured and
sent to Rome in chains. Still later, Hengist and
Horsa, the Saxon generals, imposed the most humili-
ating conditions upon the Britons, to which they were
compelled to submit. Then came William of Normandy, defeated Harold at Hastings, and the blood
of the most renowned land-pirates and sea-robbers
that ever disgraced humanity, mixed with the Briton
and Saxon, and gave to the world the Anglo-Saxon
race, with its physical ability, strong mind, brave
and enterprising spirit. And, yet, all that this race
is, it owes to its mixed blood. Civilization, or the
social condition of man, is the result and test of the
qualities of every race. The benefit of this blood
mixture, the negro is never to enjoy on this conti-
nent. In the South where he is raised, in the North,
East, or West, it is all the same, no new blood is to
be infused into his sluggish veins.

His only hope is education, **professions, trades,**

and copying the best examples, no matter from what source they come.

This antipathy to amalgamation with the negro, has shown itself in all of the States. Most of the Northern and Eastern State Legislatures have passed upon this question years ago. Since the coming in of the present year, Rhode Island's Senate refused to repeal the old law forbidding the intermarriage of whites and blacks. Thus the colored man is left to "paddle his own canoe" alone. Where there is no law against the mixture of the two races, there is a public sentiment which is often stronger than law itself. Even the wild blood of the red Indian refuses to mingle with the sluggish blood of the negro. This is no light matter, for race hate, prejudice and common malice all die away before the melting power of amalgamation. The beauty of the half-breeds of the South, the result of the crime of slavery, have long claimed the attention of writers, and why not a lawful mixture? And then this might help in

> " Making a race far more lovely and fair,
> Darker a little than white people are:
> Stronger, and nobler, and better in form,
> Hearts more voluptuous, kinder, and warm;
> Bosoms of beauty, that heave with a pride
> Nature had ever to white folks denied."

Emigration to other States, where the blacks will come in contact with educated and enterprising whites, will do them much good. This benefit by commercial intercourse is seen in the four thousand colored people who have come to Boston, where most of them are employed as servants. They are sought after as the best domestics in the city. Some of these people, who were in slavery before the war, are now engaged in mercantile pursuits, doing good business, and showing what contact will do. Many of them rank with the ablest whites in the same trades. Indeed, the various callings are well represented by Southern men, showing plainly the need of emigration. Although the colored man has been sadly at fault in not vindicating his right to liberty, he has, it is true, shown ability in other fields. Benjamin Banneker, a negro of Maryland, who lived a hundred years ago, exhibited splendid natural qualities. He had a quickness of apprehension, and a vivacity of understanding, which easily took in and surmounted the most subtile and knotty parts of mathematics and metaphysics. He possessed in a large degree that genius which constitutes a man of letters; that quality without which judgment is cold, and knowledge is inert; that energy which collects, combines, amplifies, and animates.

The rapid progress made in acquiring education and homesteads by the colored people of the South, in the face of adverse circumstances, commends the highest admiration from all classes.

The product of their native genius and industry, as exhibited at county and State Agricultural Fairs, speak well for the race.

At the National Fair, held at Raleigh, N. C., in the autumn of 1879, the exhibition did great credit to the colored citizens of the South, who had the matter in charge. Such manifestations of intellectual and mechanical enterprise will do much to stimulate the people to further development of their powers, and higher facilities.

The colored people of the United States are sadly in need of a National Scientific Association, to which may be brought yearly reports of such investigations as may be achieved in science, philosophy, art, philology, ethnology, jurisprudence, metaphysics, and whatever may tend to *unite* the race in their moral, social, intellectual and physical improvement.

We have negro artists of a high order, both in painting and sculpture; also, discoverers who hold patents, and yet the world knows little or nothing about them. The time for the negro to work out his destiny has arrived. Now let him show himself equal to the hour.

In this work I frequently used the word "Negro," and shall, no doubt, hear from it when the negro critics get a sight of the book. And why should I not use it? Is it not honorable? What is there in the word that does not sound as well as "English," "Irish," "German," "Italian," "French?"

"Don't call me a negro; I'm an American," said a black to me a few days since.

"Why not?" I asked.

"Well, sir, I was born in this country, and I don't want to be called out of my name."

Just then, an Irish-American came up, and shook hands with me. He had been a neighbor of mine in Cambridge. When the young man was gone, I inquired of the black man what countryman he thought the man was.

"Oh!" replied he, "he's an Irishman."

"What makes you think so?" I inquired.

"Why, his brogue is enough to tell it."

"Then," said I, "why is not your color enough to tell that you're a negro?"

"Arh!" said he, "that's a horse of another color," and left me with a "Ha, ha, ha!"

Black men, don't be ashamed to show your colors, and to own them.